DEAD FAMOUS

HENRY VIII
AND HIS CHOPPING BLOCK

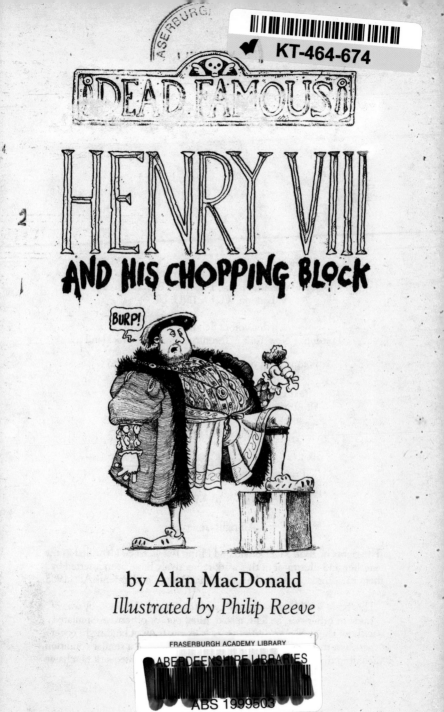

BURP!

by Alan MacDonald
Illustrated by Philip Reeve

Scholastic Children's Books,
Commonwealth House, 1–19 New Oxford Street,
London WC1A 1NU, UK

a division of Scholastic Ltd
London ~ New York ~ Toronto ~ Sydney ~ Auckland

Published in the UK by Scholastic Ltd, 1999

Text copyright © Alan MacDonald, 1999
Illustrations copyright © Philip Reeve, 1999

ISBN 0 590 11408 5

Typeset by M Rules
Printed and bound by Bath Press, Bath.

2 4 6 8 10 9 7 5 3 1

CONTENTS

Introduction   5

Timeline: The golden years   7

Growing Henry   9

Henry the hunk   32

Timeline: The troubled years   48

Holy Henry   50

Henry the hero   73

Arty Henry   103

Timeline: The rotten years   129

Hooligan Henry   130

Has-been Henry   157

INTRODUCTION

Henry VIII. Everybody has heard of him. Ask anyone why Henry is dead famous and they'll probably say. . .

HE WAS BIGGER THAN A DOUBLE-DECKER BUS!

HE GOT MARRIED SIX TIMES!

HE CHOPPED OFF MORE HEADS THAN A CHICKEN FARMER!

That's the trouble with being dead famous. People think they know all about you. But the truth is sometimes a lot more interesting than you might think. For instance, let's look at those dead famous facts again.

'Henry was fantastically fat.' Everyone knows that. But do they know that he didn't start that way? At the start Henry was dead famous for being a handsome hunk. Not only that, he was the king of fashion, the sporting superstar of his day and the writer of many

Tudor chart-toppers. This book tells you the real truth about Henry. Read his secret diary based on the real facts to find out how Henry might have felt as he went from pin-up prince to blubber mountain.

'Henry had six wives.' Everyone knows that. But do they know what his wives were really like? For instance, which wife did Henry reckon was a witch? And which one didn't recognize him on their first date? What about the wife who asked for a practice run the night before she got the chop? Turn to the pages of *The Tudor Tatler* to read the real facts about Henry's wives as a newspaper of today might have reported them (watch out for the *italic* quotes which tell you what they *really* said).

'Henry had an impressive head collection.' Everyone knows that. But do they know why the chop was preferable to some Tudor punishments we could name. Or why you should *never* pray for rain when you're going to be burnt at the stake? In this book you can get some useful tips on dying nicely from Henry's head executioner. You'll also meet Henry's headless victims and hear *their* side of the story!

It's a nasty tale full of battles, blood, betrayal, and heads on sticks.

HAVE **YOU** GOT THE STOMACH TO READ IT?

Then here's the *real* truth about Henry VIII . . . and his chopping block.

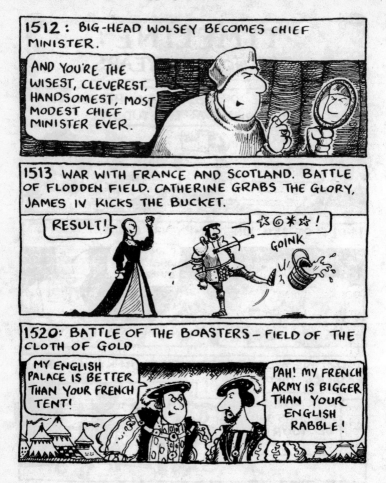

GROWING HENRY

Tudors, traitors and singing teachers

You've probably seen pictures of Henry VIII. He was a big man in many ways. Henry can claim the biggest bottom ever to flatten the throne of England. His waist grew to a button-bursting 142 centimetres (56 inches). In the bath he looked like a Tudor version of the *Titanic*. His size isn't surprising when you consider Henry's huge appetite – lunch started at 11 o'clock and went on for several hours.

Yes, Henry was a big king in every way. Big belly, big ideas and a big-head. But he didn't start off that way. He started out like this. . .

OOGLE!

On 28 June 1491 an ear-shattering wail was heard in the royal palace at Greenwich. This was Henry's first line in history. It probably meant 'off with her head'. The midwife had just stuck him in a bath and sprinkled him with rose-water to make him smell nice.

After he was christened the baby prince was kept in

GRANDMA BEAUFORTE – A RIGHT BATTLE-AXE

DAD – HENRY VII, FIRST TUDOR TO GRAB THE THRONE

HENRY

MR & MRS TUDOR

the nursery. His mum didn't feed or bath him, there was a nurse to do that.

What sort of family was Henry born into? As you probably know they were called Tudors. A family portrait when Henry was six years old might have looked a bit like this.

MUM - ELIZABETH OF YORK

BIG BROTHER - ARTHUR (11) NEXT IN LINE TO BE KING

BABY SIS - MARY (1)

BIG SIS - MARGARET (8)

WITH GRANNY AND THE KIDS.

Henry's dad, Henry VII, was the first Tudor to be king. The Tudors were a pretty weird bunch. When little Henry looked back through his family album, he'd have met some odd characters.

Henry's family album – Part 1.

Catherine of France (Great-grandma)

Catherine married King Henry V. Without her the Tudors' dodgy claim to the throne wouldn't have existed. When her first hubby died Catherine was left a lonely, 21-year-old widow. One day she found out that one of her ladies-in-waiting was stealing secret kisses from her wardrobe clerk. Catherine was hopping mad.

How dare anyone enjoy secret kisses when she wasn't! Catherine went to meet the wardrobe clerk herself to give him a piece of her mind. Instead she fell in love and gave him her hand in marriage. The wardrobe clerk was none other than Henry's great-grandad. . .

Owen Tudor (Great-grandad)

Great-grandad Owen was a nobody before his marriage. Low-born servants weren't supposed to go round proposing to queens of England. Owen's marriage caused a big scandal. He was thrown in prison and Catherine sent away to a convent. Later Owen was released and got a nice job as a park-keeper. (It beat looking after wardrobes.) Owen and Catherine got back together again and had four children. One of them was Edmund Tudor, Henry VIII's grandad.

Catherine already had a son from her first marriage to Henry V. He was. . .

Henry VI (Half great-uncle)

People said Henry VI was a crawler. Well, he was only eight months old when he came to the throne! Even when he grew up Henry made a hopeless king. He was soft in the head. At one point poor old Henry went completely bonkers for over a year. He didn't move a muscle for hours on end and couldn't even remember who he was. While Henry was playing statues, his wife, Queen Margaret, gave birth to a son, Edward. Henry didn't know anything about little Eddy until he recovered months later.

Because Henry was such a wash-out, the powerful nobles saw their chance to get their dirty hands on England's crown. That started a violent quarrel known as the Wars of the Roses.

Henry VII (Dad)

Henry VIII's dad was clever and ambitious. He wanted the crown of England for the Tudors. Never mind that there were at least ten people in England who had a better claim to the throne than him! When Henry at last grabbed the crown he spent the rest of his life worrying that he might lose it again. His motto was 'hang on to the crown even if it hangs on a bush'. Henry's determination was learned from his tough childhood. Growing up during the Wars of the Roses, he hadn't had an easy life. When it came to telling hard luck stories, Henry was the all-England champion!

HOUSE OF YORK

EMBLEM: WHITE ROSE
KINGS: EDWARD IV
        RICHARD III

THRRP!

The Wars of the Roses

The Wars of the Roses sounds like a gardening contest. Actually it was one of the bloodiest wars in English history. The two most powerful families in England – the Yorks and the Lancasters – fought each other for the crown of England. Most fights are over quickly but this one went on for *thirty years!* Before it ended, three kings had come to nasty ends – Henry VI (got the chop), young Edward V (probably murdered with his brother in the Tower of London) and Richard III (butchered at the battle of Bosworth).

Henry VII only became king because of a dirty trick. At the Battle of Bosworth, Henry had an army of 5,000 men. His enemy, Richard III, boasted an army of 18,000 men. Henry's army was outnumbered more than three to one. It looked like

16

another hard-luck story for Henry, so how on earth did he win?

Richard was betrayed by one of his scheming nobles. Almost half his army belonged to Lord Stanley (who'd married Henry's widowed mum, Margaret of Beaufort). At the key moment of the battle Stanley waited on the sidelines, making up his mind who to support.

Henry rode towards him to appeal for his help. Richard saw his plan and galloped down the hill to cut him off. At that moment Stanley finally decided – and attacked Richard. That swung the odds in Henry's favour. Richard was beaten by his nobles' treachery – and by his own barminess. He insisted on wearing his crown into battle. That made him as easy to spot as an elephant in a bun shop. Result? He got his loaf sliced.

HOUSE OF LANCASTER

EMBLEM: RED ROSE
KING: HENRY VII

GRRR!

17

Henry VII's smartest victory was away from the battlefield. He married Elizabeth of York. That meant the Yorkists and Lancastrians were on the same side. The red rose and the white rose were joined together. They could have made a pink rose. But that might have started the squabbling all over again.

So instead their new emblem was a red and white rose. Like this.

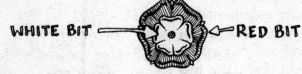

Stingy Henry

Henry VII's crown wasn't the only thing he wanted to hang on to. He also hated parting with his money. Henry was as tight as a clam. He imposed hefty taxes on his subjects because he said 'riches would only make them rich and haughty'. Fat chance with Henry VII around! Whenever one of his nobles got too rich, Henry accused them of some imaginary crime. Then they had to pay him a whopping great fine for the rest of their lives.

When he wasn't counting his taxes Henry kept up his hobby. It was called alchemy. He was convinced he could find a way to turn ordinary metal into gold and make himself as rich as a king. Of course he was as rich as a king already but that didn't stop him being greedy for more.

In 1486 Henry's first son Arthur was born and Henry ordered great celebrations throughout the land. Arthur was expected to become the next Tudor king of England. He was the apple of his daddy's eye. When little Henry came along, no one made a big fuss. He was only on the reserve list. Who could have guessed that Henry, not big brother Arthur, would become one of England's most famous kings?

Henry VII's secret diary

14 Sept. 1486

God be praised! Let every true Englishman rejoice! Today my son Arthur was born. One day he shall sit like his great father on the throne.

"Let us spare no expense, for this is a great day," I told my wife Elizabeth. "I've sent messengers galloping through the land to spread the news to every city in my kingdom." (Cost – 10 shillings. V. expensive.)

GALLOP GALLUP

In every church the bells will ring out. (Cost – nothing. A goodly custom.)

The choir at Winchester Cathedral have been ordered to sing a special mass in Latin. (Cost – 5 shillings. Choir master wanted 6 but I beat him down.)

Bonfires are being lit in every street so that the common folk can share in our happiness. (Cost-nothing. Another fine custom I shall preserve!)

The Court poets, Carmeliano and Gigli, are to celebrate the birth with Latin verses. (Cost — 7 shillings a piece. Who needs long poems?)

Elizabeth wants to build a new chapel in Winchester Cathedral to mark the occasion. It will bear her coat of arms and be a marvellous great monument admired by the whole world. On second thoughts it would also be very costly - maybe I can persuade her to light a few candles instead...

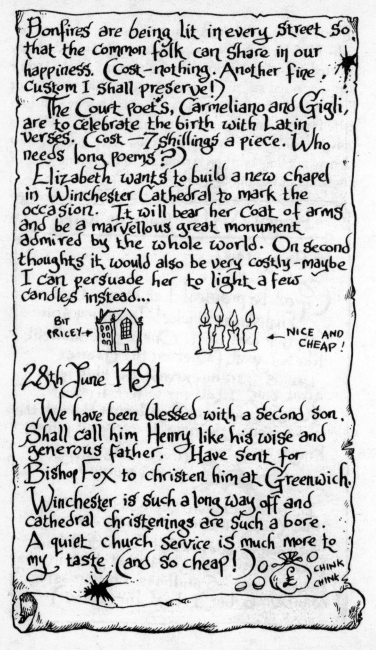

BIT PRICEY →

← NICE AND CHEAP!

28th June 1491

We have been blessed with a second son. Shall call him Henry like his wise and generous father. Have sent for Bishop Fox to christen him at Greenwich. Winchester is such a long way off and cathedral christenings are such a bore. A quiet church service is much more to my taste (and so cheap!)

CHINK CHINK

Plots and pretenders

While Henry junior was growing up, his family was constantly surrounded by danger. Henry VII could never sit comfortably on the throne. The Yorkists, still fuming at losing the Wars of the Roses, weren't giving up easily. They put up two pretenders – Lambert Simnel and Perkin Warbeck – to claim the crown for the House of York. (A pretender was someone who 'pretended' to be the rightful king. If they succeeded, they weren't pretending any more.)

Henry saw off both his rivals but they weren't the only danger. Even churchmen got mixed up in murky plots to remove the King. In 1496 a group of traitors including the Archdeacon of London were arrested. The doomed deacon probably went to the block, no one really knows. But here's the confession he might have written:

21

FOR THE CHOP:
THE ARCHDEACON OF LONDON

I, the undersigned, confess that I was drawn into a plot to kill the King. On my honour I never meant to carry out the murder myself. I was tricked by a lying magician. He is the man Your Majesty should blame. I'm only guilty of great foolishness which, grovelling on my knees, I beg Your Majesty to pardon. I had heard of a great sorcerer in Rome. So I decided to visit him, just out of curiosity, of course. While we were talking, the sorcerer showed me some ointment. He vowed it was a deadly charm.

'For instance,' said he, 'if you were to spread this ointment round a door and the King came through that door, he would die instantly.'

'How so?' I asked (shocked at the very thought).

'The magic would work on those who love him best,' he smiled toothlessly. 'They would turn pale, draw their daggers and murder the King most foully on the spot.'

I begged him to sell me the charm. Not — heaven forbid! — so that I could use it myself. I only wished to prevent it getting into the wrong hands.

Back in England my friends and I decided to test the charm's power. (Just so we could report it to the King's guard.) We chose a door in the palace when Your Majesty was out hunting. Then we spread the magic ointment around the door-frame and waited to see what would happen.

Unlucky hour! Your Majesty walked in at that moment! To my horror you passed through the very door. Your best-loved courtiers stepped forward to greet you. Trembling, I hid my eyes. But heaven smiled on you. The foul murder never took place. No one turned pale or drew a dagger. They laughed and kissed you on the cheek. The deadly charm was a rotten fake. I thanked heaven on bended knee that our beloved King was spared.

False villains have claimed we plotted all along to kill Your Majesty and were taken in by the sorcerer. It is all lies! I am your humble and true subject. Prostrating myself in the dust, I crave your pardon.

Signed by my own hand,

The Archdeacon of London.

Henry's collection

Against this background of plots and threats little Henry was growing up. He was also growing in importance. By the age of two he had started on his collection. Most children collect stamps or football stickers. Henry preferred to collect titles.

The more titles you had the more of a big noise you were. And Henry, even as a tot, was a very big noise.

Henry's family album Part 2

1493 Baby's first title

Two-year-old Henry greets the news that he's been made Constable of Dover Castle by wearing a plate of soup on his head.

1494 Baby's first knightly bath

Three-year-old Henry is led off to Westminster on a great warhorse. He is undressed by the King's counsellors and dunked in warm scented water. This makes him a Knight of the Bath. The King knights him with his sword and tells him to be 'a good knight'. Henry is then stood on the table so that everyone can see what a smart boy he is.

1494 Henry's first pair of spurs

Henry gets a thousand pounds a year to spend on romper suits as the new Duke of York. The title is a clever move by Dad to see off Perkin Warbeck. Warbeck also claims to be the Duke of York.

1495 Henry's first garter

Henry becomes a Knight of the Garter. Only the top knights are in the garter club. They are meant to be like the knights of King Arthur. (At four, Henry is a bit young for slaying dragons.)

1504 Henry's first horoscope

At 13, Henry becomes Prince of Wales. He is presented with his horoscope in Latin. It predicts he will be a devout churchman, a triumphant ruler and the father of many sons. As predictions go, this scores 1 out of 10.

Court capers

What kind of childhood did young Henry have? Some stories say he was kept under lock and key by his mean, miserly dad. One observer reckoned Henry was only allowed out through a door into a park, and even then, never by himself. This may have been true – especially since Henry VII saw plots lurking in every corner. Still, as Henry grew older, we know he was allowed to enter court life. If we could sneak a glance at his personal diary, we'd find it was an exciting time for a young prince.

Henry's secret diary (Age 7)

What a time I'm having! Court is full of goodly lords and ladies. They all bow to me and call me 'My lord, Duke of York'. I find this much to my liking. Sometimes I go out of the room and re-enter several times so they can say it again.

I played at dice with some of my lords. Somehow they kept losing and I kept winning. If the dice rolled low, I'd say, 'I wasn't ready that time', and they'd have to let me roll again! 'Fie, my lord Duke of York,' they said. 'You are much too clever for us. We cannot beat the king's son.' At last their purses were empty so we ended the game. They almost seemed glad to see me go!

Dad is always laying on marvellous pastimes to keep me amused. Today we had morris dancers and acrobats, a magician and a girl who balanced on a high wire. I pushed her off and made everyone roar with laughter! Dad also brings fools and freaks to Court for me to see. Today we had 'the great woman of Flanders'. Talk about fat — glad I'll never end up like that!

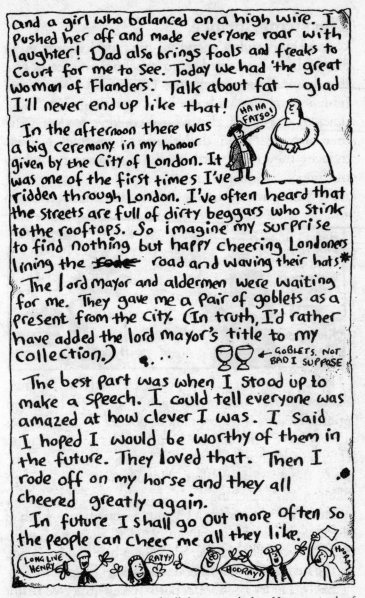

In the afternoon there was a big ceremony in my honour given by the City of London. It was one of the first times I've ridden through London. I've often heard that the streets are full of dirty beggars who stink to the rooftops. So imagine my surprise to find nothing but happy cheering Londoners lining the ~~road~~ road and waving their hats.*

The lord mayor and aldermen were waiting for me. They gave me a pair of goblets as a present from the city. (In truth, I'd rather have added the lord mayor's title to my collection.)

The best part was when I stood up to make a speech. I could tell everyone was amazed at how clever I was. I said I hoped I would be worthy of them in the future. They loved that. Then I rode off on my horse and they all cheered greatly again.

In future I shall go out more often so the people can cheer me all they like.

* The beggars had been cleared off the streets before Henry arrived, of course.

The swotty prince

Young Henry didn't spend all his time living it up at court. He was expected to go to school and learn. Not that lessons were much like they are at your school (unless your timetable includes wrestling). In Tudor times most boys of Henry's age couldn't read or write their own name. Girls didn't go to school at all. Nobody thought they were worth educating since boys did all the 'important' jobs.

Of course, Henry was a prince so his education was in another class. In fact he was in a class all by himself.

Henry's teacher was a priest called John Skelton. Skelton wasn't like most teachers or even like most priests. He was the most famous poet of his day. He was also pretty clever at insults. His congregation complained that his sermons belonged more on the stage than in the pulpit. Nobody fell asleep when Skelton was preaching.

Henry's teacher made a big impression on him. Both of them were bold, boisterous and loud. Skelton also taught the Prince a love of music. Sometimes he picked up a lute in the middle of a lesson and sang one of his poems.

Sadly, Henry's school reports haven't survived. But we know what subjects he took...

SCHOOL REPORT

NAME: Henry, my Lord Duke of York, etc. etc.
CLASS: Royal 1
FORM TEACHER: Sarky Skelton

SUBJECT:	REMARKS:
Latin and French:	Improving. The language of the gods is less like the mangling of the dogs these days.
Mathematics:	Question: If my lady hath three oranges, six hams, and five fish how many courses hath she? Answer: None. Henry hath scoffed the lot.
Logic:	Flawless. He knows he is bigger than me.
Writing:	Finds it 'tedious and painful'. In truth, like teaching princes.
Arms:	Two, and he knoweth how to use them.
Hunting:	Must have care where he pointeth his arrows
Chivalry:	Desires to become a great Knight. Will do so if his appetite grows apace.
Wrestling:	The physician has hopes of putting my shoulder back in...
Music and Dancing:	Shows a rare interest in his work. Especially the dark-haired lady.
Astronomy:	A star pupil.
General Comments:	'A boy noble in the nobility of his father, and furthermore a brilliant pupil' *

*These are Skelton's actual words. He may have been flattering Henry a teeny bit.

Step forward Henry

In 1502 something happened which changed Henry's life for ever. Arthur died. Henry's big brother, you remember, was next in line for the throne. It was bad news for his bride, Catherine of Aragon. The couple were still on their honeymoon at the time. One week he was dancing with Catherine, the next he was dead as a flat-footed dodo. No one knew the reason. Some doctors said the plague, some blamed other illnesses. Tudor doctors always said something. They didn't want to admit that they hadn't a clue.

Arthur's death meant two things for Henry. First and most importantly, he would be the next king. Second, Arthur's bride – Catherine of Aragon – was short of a husband.

THEY'RE FRESH OUT OF ARTHURS. HOW ABOUT THIS NICE HENRY INSTEAD?

Arthur died in April. Only a few weeks later the Spanish king – Catherine's father – was making plans to marry Catherine off to Henry. Maybe this sounds a bit hasty. Henry was only ten years old at the time. Catherine was an older woman (she was 16!). What's more she couldn't speak a word of English, while Henry didn't speak any Spanish. The only thing the two had in common was Arthur – and he'd been very quiet since his death.

In spite of these minor drawbacks, Henry and Catherine were married seven years later. Royal marriages were decided by politics not love. England and Spain were two powerful countries. They both hated France. What better reason for the next king of England to marry a Spanish princess?

By 1509 it was important for Henry to marry quickly. Henry VII was dying. On 20 April young prince Henry was called to his father's bedside. The King held on for another 27 hours (probably worried about his funeral bill). But finally he breathed his last. Three months before his 18th birthday, the Prince of Wales became King Henry VIII of England.

AND A MORE NOBLE, KIND AND MERCIFUL KING HAS NEVER LIVED...

HENRY THE HUNK

Court, sport and the golden years

As a teenager Henry was charming, sporty and handsome. In fact he was a bit of a hunk. He could play the lute, write pretty ditties, hunt, win a joust, dance till dawn and turn the head of any woman at court (chopping off heads came later). England was overjoyed to see the young prince on the throne.

Henry VIII was crowned in style. Two weeks before his coronation he married Catherine of Aragon. Henry said the marriage was his dad's dying wish. An alliance with Spain made sense but it's likely headstrong Henry fancied Catherine anyway. He later said. . .

> *If I were still free, I would still choose her for wife above all others.*

32

In 1509 Henry was 17 and looked something like this:

1.83M TALL (OVER 6FT), A GIANT OF HIS DAY. AVERAGE MALE HEIGHT ONLY 1.6M

LARGE BRAIN - BY ROYAL STANDARDS.

RED HAIR - WORN OVER KINGLY EARS.

ROVING EYE - FOR SPOTTING A DAINTY DAME.

CLEAN SHAVEN - BEARDS NOT YET TRENDY.

PALE SKIN - SUNTANS UNCOOL WITH TUDORS.

ARTISTIC HANDS - TO PLAY AND COMPOSE MUSIC.

SLIM WAIST - ROOM FOR SPARE TYRE

SHAPELY LEGS - FOR DANCING AND SHOWING OFF.

BIG FEET - TO TRAMPLE ANYONE WHO GETS IN THE WAY.

On 23 June he rode through the streets of London to Westminster with his new bride. Henry wanted his subjects to get a good look at him. His gold coat was studded with diamonds, rubies and emeralds. No one needed to ask, 'Which one is the King?' Henry would have made a peacock blush.

Catherine followed behind, carried on a curtained bed called a litter. Cheering crowds lined the streets. The truth was Henry's subjects *loved* him. They were queuing up to sing the new king's praises.

Getting down to work

Once Henry became king you'd think his life would have changed. Instead of hunting and dancing, there'd be meetings and lots of boring laws to pass. Not likely! Henry had no intention of changing his ways. He left politics to his ministers while he got on with more important things – like having fun!

Funnily enough his subjects didn't seem to mind. In fact it made Henry more popular – people liked to see a king who lived it up and ate like a hungry hog. It also meant it wasn't Henry's fault if the taxes were too heavy. The King wasn't to blame, he was out hunting!

In the early years of his reign Henry lived life at a terrific pace. He got up late, went to bed late and made the most of the hours in between.

A typical day in his diary might have looked like this. . .

Henry's Secret Diary

8 a.m. Yawn! Dragged myself out of bed after another late night. My pals arrived for my dressing ceremony. It's too boring to get dressed in the morning by myself. Many goodly jokes about how much we ate and drank last night.

9 a.m. Went to chapel to say my prayers. The Archbishop says good Christian kings are meant to attend mass five times a day. I've told the old goat I can only manage three times on hunting days. Lucky for me nearly every day is a hunting day!

WILD BOAR

9.30am. Saddle up. Got through eight horses today while out hunting. Why do the nags tire so easily? I'm never tired while the chase is on. Today we followed the trail of a boar for 30 miles through fields and forests. I swear I'd happily hunt all day if it wasn't for my other love calling me home. No, not Catherine...

REALLY WILD BOAR

6p.m. ...SUPPER! Ate an enormous meal of seven courses washed down with plenty of red wine. Everyone listened agog while I told them the exciting story of how I nearly killed a boar today.

7p.m. The usual messengers have been waiting all day with 'important' 'state letters' for me. I make my knaves wait till I've kicked off my muddy boots and eaten my fill. Spent a tiresome hour listening to my secretary read reports from other kingdoms. Writing replies in even worse!

WILD BORE

BLAH BLAH BLAH

I have to copy out the letters my secretary has prepared in my own handwriting. By my oath, I'd rather wrestle the King of Spain than write him a letter!

8p.m Bring on the revels! Dancing all evening with many dainty dames. I amazed everyone by dancing and leaping all evening. And this after I'd been out all day hunting!

9pm Gamble with my pals until late into the ~~tonight~~ night. I think I must have lost 40 pounds to my Lord Suffolk at dice. Who gives a fig? It all comes out of the ~~public~~ purse. What do my people pay taxes for if their king can't enjoy himself?

<u>12 midnight.</u> Crawl into bed. Another hard day governing my kingdom over.

WILD SNORE → ZZZZZ

So did Henry let the country go to the dogs while he lived it up?

Actually, no. Although he only spent an hour a day on state affairs, Henry was still the head man. His ministers did the boring work of drafting laws and letters, while he kept a firm hand on the reins. Sometimes he would change the wording of letters or tell an ambassador to take a different line with a foreign king. Henry knew what he wanted and at times made up his mind quickly.

The sporty king

Henry much preferred playing to politics. But he had a good excuse. Hunting wasn't just a sport in Tudor times, it was seen as a preparation for war. Listen to the opinion of Richard Pace writing in 1515:

> *By the body of God, I would sooner see my son hanged than be a bookworm. It is a gentleman's calling to be able to blow the horn, to hunt and to hawk. He should leave learning to clodhoppers.*

And Pace had taught at Oxford University!

Hunting wasn't Henry's only sporting passion, he found time for lots of others:

ANYONE FOR TENNIS, HAWKING, RIDING, JOUSTING, ARCHERY, WRESTLING AND GAMBLING?

The young King was as playful as a puppy and he loved any kind of game. One snowy day in 1519, Henry rushed outside to join his nobles, grabbing a cap off a boy to keep his ears warm. What was the rush – were they riding off to war? Of course not, Henry just wanted to have a snowball fight!

The surest way to win Henry's favour was to be an ace at sports and games. Many of Henry's closest pals such as Buckingham, Brandon and Compton were great sportsmen. But they weren't stupid. They knew it was best to let Henry win sometimes. Not that he needed much help. On the sports field Henry was king.

HENRY'S SPORTING ALBUM

HAWKING

When the weather was too wet or frosty for hunting, Henry went hawking. Hawks, peregrines and eagles were hunters like Henry himself. He fussed over them as if they were his own children.

Henry even passed a law to protect his little flock. Anyone who took a hawk's egg or baby hawk to raise at home would have the jealous King to deal with.

ARCHERY

Most Tudor men couldn't hit a barn door with an arrow. Guns had just been invented and people thought the longbow was yesterday's news. Henry disagreed. He practised with his bow and arrow till he was a regular Robin Hood. Henry could hit the bull's-eye from 200 metres. He passed a law to make his subjects follow his example and practise archery every day. This wasn't just for sport. Henry wanted skilled archers for his army. A well-aimed arrow could pierce steel armour and skilled archers could shoot six arrows per minute.

RIDING

Kings were expected to be great horsemen. Henry could handle a horse with the best. From an early age he learned to mount and dismount the horse without putting his foot in a stirrup. Next came the tricky bit – doing it in full armour.

The idea was to grab the mane of the galloping horse as it passed by. Then you had to leap into the saddle.

When he was older he had to find other ways to mount his horse.

GAMBLING

Henry loved to bet. He would wager money on anything – a wrestling match, a joust or a game of tennis. Sometimes he called for dice or cards to be brought in a silver bowl. A fortune could be won or lost in gambling at court. The King lost the equivalent of thousands of pounds a day. If you wanted to be in Henry's gang you needed a big purse.

Henry's court soon attracted other 'fun-loving' types. London was full of professional gamblers (also known as cheats). They dressed like rich gentlemen and travelled the city, cleaning out lords with more money than sense.

Henry did his best to drive professional gamblers out of his court. But it was like picking fleas off a dog's back. Every time he got rid of them, more came in to take their place.

Cheat tricks
- Weighted dice would always roll high or low.
- Cards were marked on the back with spots of ink or cut at the corners with little nicks to identify them.
- Cheats sometimes worked with an accomplice who told them their opponent's hand by signals. A woman sewing innocently near by could give signals to her partner by the speed of her needle.

JOUSTING

Jousting ranked with hunting as Henry's fave sport. In a joust, two armoured knights rode against each other with heavy lances. The idea was to clout your opponent and watch him bounce like a tin can. Lances were brittle and sometimes splintered against armour or shields. It was considered a mark of good jousting to break your lance. In one bout Henry and his cousin, the Duke of Suffolk, broke eight lances each.

How dangerous was a tournament exactly? Put it this way. You made your will before entering the lists. On one occasion Henry went thundering towards his opponent, forgetting one important detail. He hadn't closed his visor. The King was struck on the head. If the lance had entered the helmet he would have been a dead Henry. (No wonder he suffered from headaches in later life!)

I had a funny feeling that I'd forgotten something...

Another time the King was thrown off. His heavily armoured horse collapsed right on top of him. Henry was out cold for two hours. Luckily the horse was OK.

For a while after his coronation Henry tried to give up jousting. Well aware of the dangers, he wasn't sure a king should risk his precious neck. For six months he watched the thrill of the tournament from the royal box. Then he could stand it no longer. He entered a tournament in secret and was hooked again.

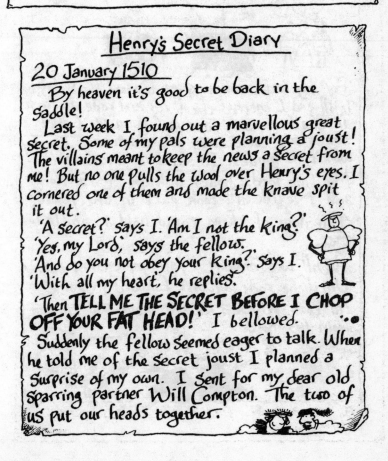

Henry's Secret Diary

20 January 1510

By heaven it's good to be back in the saddle!

Last week I found out a marvellous great secret. Some of my pals were planning a joust! The villains meant to keep the news a secret from me! But no one pulls the wool over Henry's eyes. I cornered one of them and made the knave spit it out.

'A secret?' says I. 'Am I not the king?'
'Yes, my Lord,' says the fellow.
'And do you not obey your king?' says I.
'With all my heart,' he replies.
'Then **TELL ME THE SECRET BEFORE I CHOP OFF YOUR FAT HEAD!**' I bellowed.
Suddenly the fellow seemed eager to talk. When he told me of the secret joust I planned a surprise of my own. I sent for my dear old sparring partner Will Compton. The two of us put our heads together.

43

On the day of the joust Will and I met in the hunting park at Richmond. I had a page meet us there secretly, bringing horses and arms.

Then, with our visors down, we made our entrance to the tournament. Little did anyone guess who the two unknown knights were. No one bowed to me or made way. Imagine their faces if they'd known the king of England was riding by!

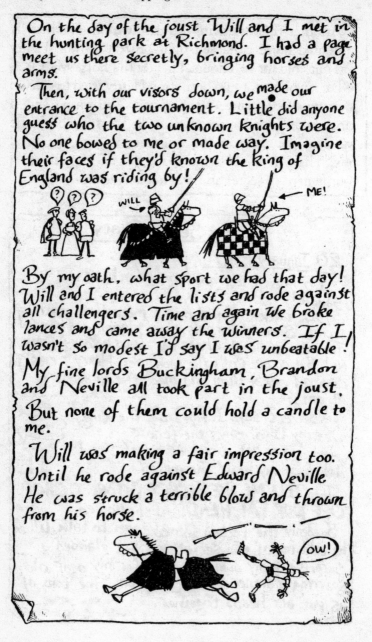

By my oath, what sport we had that day! Will and I entered the lists and rode against all challengers. Time and again we broke lances and came away the winners. If I wasn't so modest I'd say I was unbeatable!

My fine lords Buckingham, Brandon and Neville all took part in the joust. But none of them could hold a candle to me.

Will was making a fair impression too. Until he rode against Edward Neville He was struck a terrible blow and thrown from his horse.

As he was carried away I heard a doctor say he feared for Will's life. It put me in a temper I can tell you. Without my partner the fun was over. I had to quit the field.

Just as I turned to go, a voice cried out, 'God Save the King!' I was discovered! It must have been my heroic bearing that gave the game away. I lifted my visor and bowed to the cheering crowds.

They won't forget this day in a hurry. By St George! What a King sits on the throne of England! Brave, clever, skilful, valiant.... it's lucky I'm not boastful or I'd be unbearable!

25 January

Will recovered! A fig for doctors, they are all villains and liars!

Good old Harry?

There was no doubt Henry was popular early in his reign. It wasn't just that he was young and fresh on the throne. He acted the way people expected a king to act. He dressed gorgeously and lived life to the full. Even in the golden years, however, Henry had a dark side. He could be cruel and ruthless. Edmund Dudley and Sir Thomas Empson discovered that. The two nobles were trusted servants to Henry's dad. When Henry VIII became king they quickly lost their positions – and their heads.

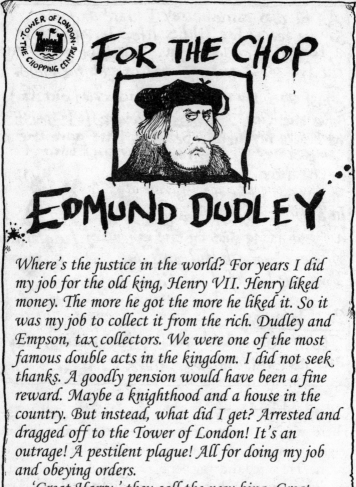

FOR THE CHOP

EDMUND DUDLEY

Where's the justice in the world? For years I did my job for the old king, Henry VII. Henry liked money. The more he got the more he liked it. So it was my job to collect it from the rich. Dudley and Empson, tax collectors. We were one of the most famous double acts in the kingdom. I did not seek thanks. A goodly pension would have been a fine reward. Maybe a knighthood and a house in the country. But instead, what did I get? Arrested and dragged off to the Tower of London! It's an outrage! A pestilent plague! All for doing my job and obeying orders.

'Great Harry,' they call the new king. Great scoundrel more like! His father must be turning somersaults in his grave. Young Henry only cares for popularity. He knew Empson and I had made enemies. People said we were lining our own purses as well as the King's. Us! Men so fair and honest

we were made MPs!

Empson and I were found guilty of treason. They sentenced us to be hung, drawn and quartered. Carved up like a couple of plucked chickens and hung out to dry. For a year Henry drew out the torture by keeping us in the Tower of London. I wrote a book to pass the time.* I even plotted my escape. Just my ill luck it was discovered.

Now our miserable lives are over. To show his great mercy, Henry let us die swiftly on the block. Thanks, Henry, you're a pal! I hope your conscience keeps you awake at night. And next time your greedy family needs any taxes collecting – do it yourself!

Edmund Dudley

* Dudley's book was called *The Tree of Commonwealth*. In it he described himself as 'the most wretched and sorrowful creature, being a dead man by the king's laws whom I never offended in treason or things like it to my knowledge.'

1533: THOMAS CROMWELL GRABS TOP SPOT AS CHIEF MINISTER. HENRY FINALLY GETS HIS DIVORCE, MARRIES WIFE NO 2 ANNE BOLEYN. DAUGHTER ELIZABETH BORN. (HENRY UNDER THE MOON).

Goo! EUGH!

1535: THOMAS MORE FOR THE CHOP.

POO!

1536: ANNE BOLEYN FOR THE CHOP. HENRY MARRIES WIFE NO. 3 JANE SEYMOUR. CATHERINE OF ARAGON DIES. PILGRIMAGE OF GRACE – THE PEASANTS ARE REVOLTING.

BOO! BOO! BOO!

1537: SON EDWARD VI BORN. JANE SEYMOUR DIES.

EUGH! GOO! COOTCHY-COOTCHY-COO!

HOLY HENRY

Divorce, ditching the Pope and dying nicely

By 1527 Henry was beginning to realize he had a big problem. It's known in history as 'the king's great matter'. Being married to Catherine wasn't so great and it mattered a lot to Henry. Here's how Henry might have described his troubles:

HENRY'S SECRET DIARY

By my oath, a pretty mess I'm in! Here I am, King of all England, without a royal son to fill my boots after I'm gone! There's a daughter, Mary, a healthy child, but what use is a girl? Whoever heard of a queen of England? Even if I left Mary my crown all the power would be in the hands of her cursed husband!

1 England had only once had a queen before, Queen Matilda – and that led to 19 years of civil war (1135–1154)! Henry feared another war if he didn't leave a son to be king. Just as bad, if Mary got married her husband might steal the crown from the Tudors.

Is this curtains for the great name of Tudor? By the devil's fork, not while I still draw breath!

It's obvious Cath is now past having children. No chance of a son there. And now I'm wild about that dainty morsel, Anne Boleyn. How I long to take her aside and kiss her sweet ducky lips!

There is only one thing for it. Ditch ugly old Cath and marry pretty young Annie. I owe it to my country! Anne will bear me a bouncing boy and England will have an heir to the throne. What could be better for everyone (especially me)?

BOING!

But here's the snag. For a divorce I must go cap in hand to that old goat, the Pope. Surely it's obvious to anyone I should never have married my brother's wife. (o.k. so it wasn't obvious to me at the time.)

I'll get my top man, crafty Cardinal Wolsey to work on the divorce. If anyone can pull it off he can. I am dying of love for my sweet Annie, my dove, my lambkin. Hurry it up, Wolsey, or heads will roll!

Pope problems

Henry's divorce was going to be no pushover. England was a Catholic country and Catholics weren't supposed to get divorced. The only person who could grant permission was the Pope. But Pope Clement VII found himself playing piggy in the middle between Henry and Emperor Charles V. The Emperor had conquered Rome and had Clement at his mercy. And it just so happened that Emperor Charlie's aunt was dead against the divorce. She was Catherine of Aragon so she would be! If the Pope refused the divorce, he angered Henry. If he didn't, he enraged the Emperor. Clement couldn't win. So he made up his mind his best policy was not to make up his mind.

A tale of four Toms – Part 1

Henry gave the job of handling the divorce to Thomas Wolsey. Throughout his life Henry relied heavily on men called Tom. Maybe all Toms were wise. Or maybe Henry just liked the name. Either way, it can get confusing remembering which Tom was which. Here's a chart to help you sort them out.

We'll meet Taxing Tom later when Henry runs into money trouble. For now, let's find out more about the three Toms who won and lost by Henry's divorce.

NAME	THOMAS WOLSEY	THOMAS MORE	THOMAS CRANMER	THOMAS CROMWELL
AKA*	BIGHEAD TOM	HONEST TOM	YES TOM	TAXING TOM
JOB	LORD CHANCELLOR	LORD CHANCELLOR	ARCHBISHOP OF CANTERBURY	LORD CHAMBERLAIN
CLAIM TO FAME	WANTED TO BE FIRST ENGLISH POPE	WROTE A FAMOUS BOOK CALLED 'UTOPIA'	FIXED HENRY'S DIVORCE	CLEANING OUT THE MONASTERIES
BIG MISTAKE	FAILING TO GET HENRY'S DIVORCE	OPPOSING THE DIVORCE	BEING A PROTESTANT	FIXING A MARRIAGE WITH UGLY ANNE OF CLEVES
STICKY END	DIED UNDER ARREST 	 THE CHOP	BURNT DURING CATHOLIC MARY'S REIGN 	THE CHOP 

* Aka = also known as

53

Thomas Wolsey – Big-head Tom

For 14 years Thomas Wolsey was second only to Henry as the most powerful man in England. He was also the most hated man in England. As a cardinal (one down from being pope) Wolsey should have been godly and humble. Instead he was a big-head and a show-off.

Wolsey got so powerful he imagined he was royalty. He boasted about his riches, and dressed in furs and red silk robes. His cardinal's hats were the finest you could buy in France. He even had his bed carved with them!

Say you visited Wolsey at his Hampton Court Palace. You might go looking for the cook to fix you a hearty supper. But you'd have trouble spotting him! Instead of an apron he went about in a velvet coat with a gold chain about his neck. Wolsey even dressed his servants like nobles.

A visitor from Venice had no doubt. 'This cardinal is king,' he said.

At the start of Henry's reign, Wolsey would tell people...

Later it became...

Before long it was. . .

That was enough to get anyone's goat. The nobles thought Wolsey had a nerve acting so high and mighty. Born a butcher's son, they reckoned he was a pork chop dressed up like a steak. Worse still, they couldn't gossip about Wolsey to each other. If their words got back to Henry, they'd be the ones for the chop!

Only one man dared speak out. That was Henry's old schoolteacher, John Skelton. He was still writing poems and insulting everybody. Skelton knew Henry would never arrest his old favourite so he was as rude as he liked. He wrote several mocking poems about the stuck-up Cardinal. A typical verse called him: 'bold', 'bragging', 'basely born', 'fat as a maggot' and 'bred of a fish fly'. And it went on like that for pages!

55

Wolsey was riding so high that sooner or later he was bound to fall. He wasn't content to be Henry's right-hand man. He wanted to become the first English pope. Funnily enough, no one else was keen on the idea! In the end his downfall was Henry's divorce. Wolsey thought he could use his influence with the Pope to get what Henry wanted. But the task proved beyond even the Great Bighead. Henry had the Cardinal arrested but sickly Wolsey died before his head ever reached the block.

The long divorce

Henry's divorce from Catherine took *six years* to achieve. According to Henry, marrying his dead brother's wife had been unlawful. Catherine pointed out he hadn't thought so at the time. In any case, the marriage had received the blessing of Pope Leo X himself. Pope Clement didn't want to say the previous Pope had been wrong. So he dithered and delayed. After six years of the dithers Henry got fed up waiting. He married Anne Boleyn in secret. Then he decided, if the Catholic church wouldn't grant his divorce, he'd start his own church. And guess who would be head of it?

Yes Tom

Henry's divorce had big consequences – and not just for his wife, Catherine. The quarrel caused a bust-up with Rome. Since the Pope wouldn't do what Henry wanted, Henry looked around for a churchman who would. Enter Thomas Cranmer.

Cranmer was made Archbishop of Canterbury so he could be Henry's yes-man. Cranmer granted the divorce and Henry made himself Head of the Church. In one clever move he got his divorce and made himself stronger. He was now free from the Pope's power and had the English church under his thumb. To this day the head of the Church of England is the king or queen.

CRANMER'S THE NAME DIVORCE IS THE GAME!

Honest Tom

The divorce was bad news for someone else. Once Wolsey got the boot, Henry turned to another Tom to be his Lord Chancellor. Thomas More was a clever thinker and writer. He was also an honest man and loyal to the Pope. He didn't support Henry's divorce or the split with Rome. For a while More tried to keep mum about his views. But soon he was heading for the chopping block.

FOR THE CHOP

TOWER OF LONDON · THE CHOPPING CENTRE

THOMAS MORE

Maybe I should have been a village idiot. Look where learning has got me! If I hadn't been so clever I might still have a head on my shoulders. It was learning that used to keep me awake at nights. In truth, it was Henry's learning. As a boy he used to barge into my room at all hours.

YAWN

'Wake up, Thomas!' he'd shout in my ear. 'I desire your good company to look at the stars.'

Yawning, I'd have to drag myself out of my warm bed. I'd have helped him to see stars most gladly. The kind you get from a good clout round the head!

When he became king, learning drew him to my house. Henry loved to discuss things. Religion, supper, music, books, supper. . . Once while we were talking, Henry put an arm round my shoulders. My son-in-law saw it and later said it was plain I was the King's favourite. I smiled. 'But if chopping my head off could win him a castle in France, he'd do it tomorrow,' I said.

And how right I was! It was my learning got me the job of Chancellor and into hot water. Henry decreed everyone had to swear an oath to him as head of the Church. What was I to do? As a true Catholic I believed the Pope was head of the Church. But to deny my king put my head on the block. Still I thought learning could save me. As a lawyer I knew a man who held his tongue could not be held a traitor.

'Do you swear the King is head of the Church?' they asked me. I said nothing.

'Do you refuse to swear?' I was silent as the grave.

'DO YOU TAKE THE OATH OR NOT?' They were yelling by now. But I kept my dumb act for days. I told you I would have made a good village idiot!

It didn't save my poor neck in the end. Someone claimed they'd heard me say Parliament had no power to make Henry head of the Church. Villainous lies! I may be too clever for my own good, but I'm not a fool!

Henry had me executed. That's gratitude for you! After all the meals he'd eaten at my house. My head was displayed on London Bridge. I hope it will be a warning to all honest men. That's where learning gets you.

Thomas More.

Thomas More's last words were:

> *Pluck up thy spirits, man, and be not afraid, my neck is very short!*

How to die nicely

Prisoners in the Tower of London had plenty of time to think about dying. Most nobles were executed on Tower Hill, a short walk away. Thomas More could probably hear the scaffold being erected the night before. It was important for a gentleman or lady to die a good death. Their friends and family would be there to see them. Large crowds also came. A day out at an execution was better than watching a football match in those days. Henry sent many nobles for the chop, so the axeman was kept in regular work. If anyone could advise on making a nice death it was Henry's chopper-in-chief.

Tips from the chopping block by B. Head

1. DIE WITH STYLE.
YOU'RE LUCKY. THERE ARE WORSE THINGS THAN HAVING YOUR HEAD CHOPPED OFF, YOU KNOW. IT'S A NOBLE'S DEATH – BETTER THAN HANGING OR BURNING ON A BONFIRE ANY DAY. ALL THAT CHOKING AND COUGHING. YOU WOULDN'T LIKE IT, I CAN TELL YOU!

SO TRY NOT TO TREMBLE WHEN YOU MOUNT THE SCAFFOLD. WORSE STILL, DON'T DRIBBLE DOWN YOUR DOUBLET OR MUTTER TO YOURSELF. THE CROWD LOVE TO SEE A NICE DEATH. YOU SHOULD DIE LIKE A GENTLEMAN. IN YEARS TO COME PEOPLE WILL SAY, 'REMEMBER THAT LORD SO-AND-SO? DIED LOVELY, DIDN'T HE? I COULD WATCH HIM POP HIS CLOGS ANY DAY OF THE WEEK!'

2. SAY YOUR PRAYERS.

DON'T FORGET TO MAKE PEACE WITH THE GOOD LORD ABOVE. AFTER ALL YOU'LL BE MEETING HIM IN A MINUTE OR TWO, (IF YOU DON'T GO TO THE OTHER PLACE). I'D PUT IN A GOOD WORD FOR YOURSELF IF I WAS YOU. ANYWAY, THE CROWD LIKE TO SEE A LORD OR A DUKE DOWN ON HIS KNEES. MAKES THEM FEEL THERE'S JUSTICE IN THE WORLD AFTER ALL.

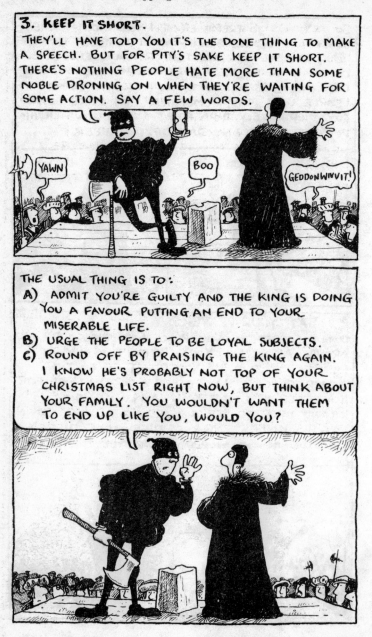

3. KEEP IT SHORT.

THEY'LL HAVE TOLD YOU IT'S THE DONE THING TO MAKE A SPEECH. BUT FOR PITY'S SAKE KEEP IT SHORT. THERE'S NOTHING PEOPLE HATE MORE THAN SOME NOBLE DRONING ON WHEN THEY'RE WAITING FOR SOME ACTION. SAY A FEW WORDS.

YAWN

BOO

GEDDONWIVIT!

THE USUAL THING IS TO:

A) ADMIT YOU'RE GUILTY AND THE KING IS DOING YOU A FAVOUR PUTTING AN END TO YOUR MISERABLE LIFE.

B) URGE THE PEOPLE TO BE LOYAL SUBJECTS.

C) ROUND OFF BY PRAISING THE KING AGAIN. I KNOW HE'S PROBABLY NOT TOP OF YOUR CHRISTMAS LIST RIGHT NOW, BUT THINK ABOUT YOUR FAMILY. YOU WOULDN'T WANT THEM TO END UP LIKE YOU, WOULD YOU?

4. REMEMBER YOUR EXECUTIONER.

I'M THE LAST PERSON YOU'LL SEE. FUNNY THAT, AIN'T IT. YOUR HEAD IS IN MY HANDS, OR IT SOON WILL BE. NOT MANY PEOPLE REALIZE THAT AN EXECUTIONER'S JOB IS SKILLED WORK. IT'S NOT JUST 'SWISH, CHOP, BUMP, BUMP.' NO, THERE'S THE SLOW WAY AND THE QUICK WAY. IF I DO A GOOD JOB, IT'S OVER NICE AND QUICK. IF I'M A BIT RUSTY (OR ME AXE IS) THEN IT CAN BE MESSY.

I'VE KNOWN EXECUTIONS TAKE THREE OR FOUR BLOWS. SOMETIMES THEY EVEN HAVE TO GET THE SAW OUT TO FINISH THE JOB. NOT A PRETTY SIGHT FOR YOUR NEAREST AND DEAREST. SO, BEARING THIS IN MIND, IT'S A GOOD IDEA TO HAVE YOUR TIP READY WHEN YOU MEET ME. GOLD IS MY SPECIAL FAVOURITE. I DO A NICE CLEAN JOB FOR A GOLD RING OR A CHAIN.

Dead ends – and dastardly punishments

Death on the chopping block wasn't the only sentence Henry could hand out. Worse things were reserved for commoners and rebels.

Hang 'im!

Thieves and murderers were usually hanged to teach them a lesson. They were left on the gallows until they were dead. Rebels were a different matter. If they rebelled against their overlord they were sometimes hung in chains that passed under their armpits. Luckily the

chains didn't kill them. Unluckily, they starved to death anyway. Rebellion against the King was treason and demanded an even worse punishment.

Have the villain hanged, drawn and quartered!

Henry passed over 70 laws against treason. They covered everything from trying to kill the King to daring to criticize his policies. The punishment was especially nasty. The victim would be hanged by the neck, then cut down before they were actually dead. A man then had his most, ahem . . . private parts cut off and his bowels removed. They were burned before his eyes. You would think this was quite grisly enough. But no. Just, to make sure, the head was cut off and the body sliced in quarters. The head and bloody body bits were fixed on a pole on London Bridge for everyone to see. Of course Henry didn't let nobles or queens die this way. After all, he didn't want people to think he was some kind of monster.

Burn the heretic!

A heretic was anyone who disagreed with the 'normal' religious beliefs of the day. Of course what was 'normal' could change. During Henry's reign it was dangerous to

be a Protestant.* When his daughter Elizabeth ruled it was just as dodgy to be a Catholic.

A public burning was a popular event. Villagers came from miles around, bringing their packed lunch with them. Before the burning got under way a priest preached a sermon. He reminded people not to listen to new religious ideas. 'You too might end up on a spit roast,' warned the preacher. After the sermon the victim

* Although England had split with Rome the Protestant Church wasn't established until later.

said goodbye to his friends. If he was lucky he might get a last cup of wine.

He had the choice to be burned in his underwear or to keep his clothes on. (Poor people often gave away their clothes – shame to get them all smoky.) The victim was then tied to a stake and bundles of wood were heaped round him. The sheriff gave the signal and the fire was lit.

Sometimes the victim's friends were allowed to hang a bag of gunpowder round his neck. This made sure the burning was quick and went with a bang. Other victims suffered a slow death. It was best to avoid rainy days: if the wood got damp it took longer to burn. One bishop took all of three quarters of an hour to die.

Henry wasn't the bonfire king. It was his daughter Mary, who was the bonfire *queen*. She burnt 280 heretics in just five years!

Heartless Henry

Henry wasn't the first king to send his enemies to the chopping block or worse. He wasn't the last either. What shocked people wasn't the number of executions, it was the names of the victims. Henry thought nothing of beheading his best friend (Thomas More), his best minister (Thomas Cromwell), his own wives (Anne Boleyn and Catherine Howard) and even a bishop (John Fisher).

One head more or less made no difference to Henry. As long as he was safe on the throne, who cared?

One person who escaped the chopping block but still came to a sinister end was Henry's first wife – Catherine of Aragon.

The Tudor Tatler

9 Jan 1536

QUEEN IN POISON DEATH DRAMA!

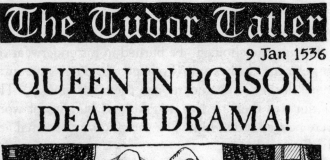

Who killed our queen?

Catherine of Aragon died yesterday amid sensational rumours that she was poisoned by the King, *writes rogue reporter, Ralph Quill.*

Her Spanish doctor claimed, 'The poison, it is a deadly potion. I am sure it is in some Welsh beer my lady is drinking. The King, he is a treacherous dog!'

El doctor

Others claim the murder was the dirty work of Anne Boleyn, the new queen. Anne has never pretended to like Catherine. She once wished that all the Spanish *'were at the bottom of the sea'*. Fishy or what?

Are the rumours true? *The Tudor Tatler* today publishes *exclusive pictures* of the King in mourning for his first wife.

Not exactly heartbroken, eh Henry? The King wore a cheery suit of yellow satin and a smug smile on his face.

Even so, the Spanish doctor may have got his prescriptions

Henry mourns our queen

muddled. Poisoning doesn't sound like Henry's style. If Henry wants someone dead he doesn't bother to do it in secret. The noose, the chop or burning at the stake, yes. Poison, no.

To the murder charge *The Tudor Tatler* says: 'Not likely, el doctor!'

To the charge that Henry broke his wife's heart we say: 'Guilty, the rat'

Consider the facts:

For 20 years Catherine was a good wife to the King

She was only 16 when she came to England. She suffered the shock of losing her first husband (Henry's big bro, Arthur) after only five months.

Did she run home to Papa? No, she waited patiently and did her duty by later marrying 18-year-old Henry.

The people's queen

Catherine may not have been a great beauty, but we English loved her. We loved her long red hair and tiny doll-like hands and feet. We loved her because she was clever,

Cathy: national treasure

69

talented and fearless.

When Henry was off fighting in France, who did he leave as captain-general of the army? None other than Courageous Cathy.

What a heroine

When the Scots invaded England, Cathy rallied her troops. She ordered the Earl of Surrey into battle and marched north herself with an army in support. If needs be plucky Cath would have fought herself – never mind that she was about to give birth! Luckily Surrey won the Battle of Flodden before she arrived. The credit still went to Cathy. Who else would have sent Henry the bloody shirt of his dead enemy, James IV?

Thoughtful or what?

She was a hit with Henry

Has the King forgotten the days when he was mad about his first wife? Look at this poem he wrote about her:

'As the holly groweth green,
And never changeth hue,
so I am, ever hath been,
unto my lady true.'

Nice rhyme, Henry, pity about the whopping lie!

Catherine tried to be a good mother

Henry wanted a son to make sure he kept the throne in the family. And no one can say that Catherine didn't try. She gave birth six times. It wasn't her fault that only one child –

Cathy – odd taste in shirts

Mary – one out of six

Mary – lived more than a few weeks. After six pregnancies Henry then had the cheek to complain that the Queen was losing her figure!

The divorce was a fix

When Henry got the hots for sizzling Anne Boleyn he wanted an excuse to divorce Catherine. And what did he come up with? He suddenly decided it was wrong to have married his brother's wife – 20 years after the wedding! Come off it, Henry, who are you kidding?

Catherine got the boot

So Cathy, who spent half her life in prayer, died as poor as a nun. The last words she wrote to her ungrateful husband were:

'*I make this vow, mine eyes desire you above all things. Farewell!*'

Did Henry weep tears of regret? Did he get down on his knees to beg his wife's pardon? Not likely! Heartless Henry wouldn't even let her be buried in St Paul's Cathedral. He was worried it would cost him too much!

THE TATLER COMMENT

It's time to stop the rot, Henry! Once you had the whole country behind you, now you're going off the rails! Cathy didn't deserve to be chucked in the bin like yesterday's dinner. She was a good queen and a good wife. *The Tatler* only hopes Anne Boleyn doesn't live to regret being your second choice.

Bright future for wife

When it came to wife swapping or head chopping Henry wasn't exactly holy. But it didn't change his high opinion of himself. Henry still thought of himself as a hero. And there was only one way to prove it to the rest of the world. It involved swords, armour, arrows, cannons and buckets of blood...

HENRY THE HERO

Boasts, battles and barmy armies

> *The common folk do not go to war of their own accord but are driven to it by the madness of kings.*

Thomas More

All Henry's tournaments and archery contests were really just rehearsals. He was practising for the real thing – war. Henry would fight anyone. The French. The Scots. The Spanish. He dreamt of writing his name in the history books as England's most glorious warrior-king. Nowadays most people agree war is a waste of good people. But in Henry's day a king who never went to war was a bit of a softy. Henry saw it as a chance to cover himself in glory.

> *My ambition is not merely to equal but to excel the glorious deeds of my ancestors.*

As a boy Henry's bedtime stories weren't about cuddly teddies or fluffy bunnies. He preferred to read about knights in shining armour slicing off giants' heads. Henry's heroes were King Arthur and the knights of the Round Table. He dreamed of bringing back the glorious days of chivalry when men were men and damsels were in distress. This is how he might have thought of himself.

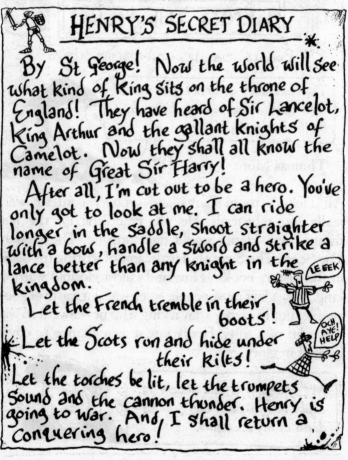

HENRY'S SECRET DIARY

By St George! Now the world will see what kind of King sits on the throne of England! They have heard of Sir Lancelot, King Arthur and the gallant knights of Camelot. Now they shall all know the name of Great Sir Harry!

After all, I'm cut out to be a hero. You've only got to look at me. I can ride longer in the saddle, shoot straighter with a bow, handle a sword and strike a lance better than any knight in the kingdom.

LE EEK

Let the French tremble in their boots!

OCH AYE! HELP

Let the Scots run and hide under their kilts!

Let the torches be lit, let the trumpets sound and the cannon thunder. Henry is going to war. And I shall return a conquering hero!

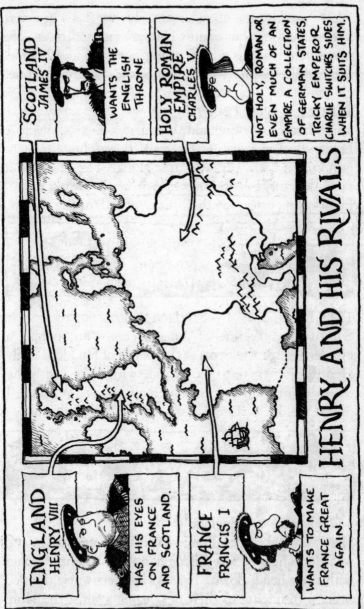

HENRY AND HIS RIVALS

SCOTLAND
JAMES IV
WANTS THE ENGLISH THRONE

HOLY ROMAN EMPIRE
CHARLES V
NOT HOLY, ROMAN OR EVEN MUCH OF AN EMPIRE. A COLLECTION OF GERMAN STATES. TRICKY EMPEROR CHARLIE SWITCHES SIDES WHEN IT SUITS HIM.

ENGLAND
HENRY VIII
HAS HIS EYES ON FRANCE AND SCOTLAND.

FRANCE
FRANCIS I
WANTS TO MAKE FRANCE GREAT AGAIN.

Well everyone has their dreams. Henry did win a few famous victories but mainly his wars just fizzled out. He never achieved his aim of ruling Scotland and France. Meanwhile, his dreams of glory cost the country a fortune.

Henry's war record

1513 France 0 – England 0

England's new manager Henry VIII watches his team grind out a boring draw against France. Henry claims a tactical victory by taking a couple of French fortress towns. English supporters say their team settled for the draw.

1513 England 'B' 1 – Scotland 0

Substitute Catherine of Aragon comes on to play a blinder against the Scots at the Battle of Flodden. Sadly Henry is not there to see his side win, as he's with the 'A' team in France. Scots supremo, James IV, says, 'I did'na see the goal myself.' He was dead by half time.

1523 France 0 – England 0

Henry's hopes of a crushing victory are frozen out by the weather. The match is called off and our lads head home with their heads down. To make matters worse, France suffer a trouncing in their next game against the Holy

Roman Empire led by rival Charles V. England boss, Henry, is said to be 'sick as a parrot'.

1528 England 0 – Holy Roman Empire 0
Henry puts out his strongest team for a home match against Charles's imperial boys. Match again called off when the Empire team fails to turn up for the invasion.

1542 England 2 – Scotland 0
Henry takes some crumbs of comfort from another victory against the Scots on a waterlogged pitch at Solway Moss.

1543 France 0 – England 0
England boss Henry heaves his huge hulk into the frontline for a last away game against the French. Sadly recent star-signing Emperor Charles V pulls out at the last minute. Ageing Henry's dodgy legs force him to board the coach home.

Verdict: A sad end to a disappointing season for England. Henry won't be collecting the Monarch of the Month Award.

The big fight

Henry's number one enemy was France. A hundred years earlier England heroic king, Henry V, had claimed the French throne. 'Hang on,' you may think, 'he wasn't French.' That didn't stop him. Royal family trees drawn up by English experts showed (guess what?) that the French throne really belonged to the English! Henry V had won a famous victory at Agincourt where his 7,000 English soldiers defeated an army three times its size.

Henry VIII saw himself following in his namesake's footprints. He dreamed of glorious victories and revived the old English claim to France as his excuse.

Henry's big rival was another king keen to make a name for himself. Francis I of France. The two young rulers both wanted to be to number one in Europe. Henry had his dreams of glory and his eye on the French throne. Francis aimed to restore the lands France had lost.

Henry didn't trust Francis. He once said:

I know for certain that he wishes me worse than the devil himself.

He had good reason for suspecting the French. A spy sent back a disturbing report from France in 1519. It went something like this.

Top Secret - for the King's eyes only

Your great and most noble majesty,

Yesterday I came upon the King of France, riding along the road from Lyons. He was deep in conversation with a companion. Your Majesty will not be surprised to learn it was the English traitor, Richard De la Pole. The very same upstart who lays claim to your throne and broods like a viper in France, waiting his chance to strike. What they were discussing I found out later from a servant. (A silver coin soon loosens the tongue.)

Francis and Pole plan to send four assassins to the English court. There, by crafty means, they are to set fire to the palace where Your Grace is sleeping. Their object is to murder you in your bed and anyone else in the palace at the time. For this act of treachery, Pole promised the villains a reward of four thousand francs.

Be on your guard, my lord, and do not trust that cunning fox Francis. He smiles while holding a dagger behind his back.

Your faithful and true spy.

(This scroll will self-destruct in 10 seconds.)

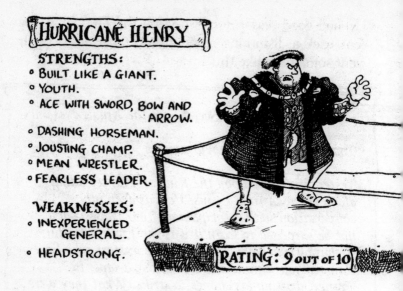

HURRICANE HENRY

STRENGTHS:
- BUILT LIKE A GIANT.
- YOUTH.
- ACE WITH SWORD, BOW AND ARROW.
- DASHING HORSEMAN.
- JOUSTING CHAMP.
- MEAN WRESTLER.
- FEARLESS LEADER.

WEAKNESSES:
- INEXPERIENCED GENERAL.
- HEADSTRONG.

RATING: 9 OUT OF 10

Henry and Francis were spoiling for a fight, and they were pretty well matched.

Battle of the boasters

But Henry and Francis didn't go to war at first. At least not with armies and weapons. Henry had already fought one campaign against Francis' father (Louis) and needed a breathing space. So, instead of all-out war, the two rival kings agreed to meet in peace. They arranged a meeting that became a battle of the boasters. It was known as the Field of the Cloth of Gold.

The meeting was to celebrate peace at last between two long-term enemies, England and France. But in truth, Henry wanted to prove he was Europe's number one and Francis planned to show him a thing or two about French style.

Preparations for a great tournament were made. The

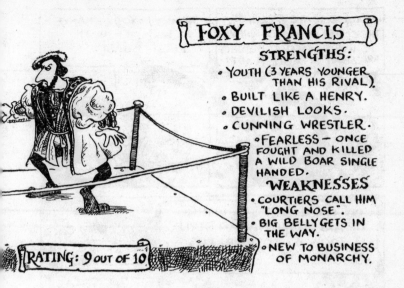

FOXY FRANCIS

STRENGTHS:
- YOUTH (3 YEARS YOUNGER THAN HIS RIVAL)
- BUILT LIKE A HENRY.
- DEVILISH LOOKS.
- CUNNING WRESTLER.
- FEARLESS — ONCE FOUGHT AND KILLED A WILD BOAR SINGLE HANDED.

WEAKNESSES
- COURTIERS CALL HIM "LONG NOSE".
- BIG BELLY GETS IN THE WAY.
- NEW TO BUSINESS OF MONARCHY.

RATING: 9 OUT OF 10

chosen place was Flanders' Golden Valley in France. Only four years before, the valley had been littered with French bodies when Henry attacked the nearby town of Ardres. It seemed hard to imagine the French and English could meet again without making a bloody mess of the countryside.

As the hot summer of 1520 went on, the valley began to look like a land of fairy castles. The two kings were set-building for a show which Hollywood would have been proud of.

News of the Field of the Cloth of Gold spread all over Europe. People called it the eighth wonder of the world. Normally 16th-century kings wasted their fortunes on going to war. But this was something new. Henry and Francis were wasting money just to show off. The event was a bit like the biggest game show in history. But who won the battle of the show-offs – Henry or Francis?

And the winner?

The Field of the Cloth of Gold lasted three whole weeks. Every day Francis threw a feast for Henry or Henry threw a feast for Francis, or Catherine had the French queen round for a spot of supper. Every day lances were shattered at the tilt-yard and swords had to be hammered back into shape. Henry himself rode six horses in one day. The horses had to retire exhausted but Henry went on jousting for hours at a time.

At the end, both sides claimed to have scored vital show-off points:

Zut alors! Henry enjoys seeing Francis beaten in a joust by English knight, Weston Brown. Francis also suffers a black eye and the indignity of having the plume sliced clean off his helmet.

1 point to Henry

Mon Dieu! In the 'My tent's bigger than your tent contest' Henry comes out on top. His mock castle had taken longer to build but he has the last laugh when Francis's grand pavilion tent is blown away towards the sea, crushing other French tents as it bounces along.

2 points to Henry

Ouch! Henry sprains his hand in the jousting.
1 point to Francis

Whoops! Francis challenges Henry to a wrestling match. Great Harry is tripped up and dumped on his

mighty backside. (Of course the English claim this is cheating.) For Henry, who fancied himself as a champion wrestler, it was a big humiliation.
2 points to Francis

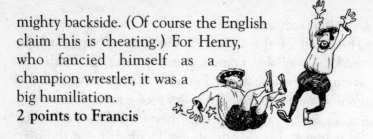

Final show-off scores: Henry 3 points – Francis 3 points

So Henry and Francis both went away happy in the end, feeling they were Europe's top dog. The two kings parted with words of great sorrow. But it was all a sham. There was never any serious attempt to bring lasting peace between France and England. Henry went straight off to meet Francis' enemy – Emperor Charles V. Together they made plans to put the upstart French in their place. The Field of the Cloth of Gold will go down as one of the greatest spectacles of the 16th century. Actually it was just two overgrown boys waving their toy swords at each other.

Henry's barmy army

Henry knew that to conquer France he would need a splendid army and navy. He spent almost a million pounds on his first French campaign alone. One of the last things he did before leaving for France in 1513 was to tighten security on his jewel house in the Tower of London. But by the time he got back there were hardly any jewels left to guard. Henry's dream of military glory cost all the money his miserly dad had saved.

Unlike some kings, Henry wanted to lead his troops into battle in person. During one seige he rode up and down in sight of the French guns wearing a gold tunic and a red feathered cap. (Just so they couldn't miss him.) Even when he was fat and fifty he was heaving himself into the saddle for another campaign. None of his generals dared to say he would only slow the army down!

Where's the beef?
An army marches on its stomach, goes the saying. But Henry's armies often marched on empty stomachs. Soldiers daily rations were:

1 POUND OF BEEF   1 POUND OF BISCUITS   1 GALLON OF BEER

This wasn't stingy. A gallon of beer is like drinking 8 pints of milk – only much stronger! The trouble started once the army left England. Then the food and drink often ran out. Greedy soldiers sometimes grabbed double or triple rations. Discipline was so bad nobody stopped them. Food wagons mysteriously vanished, animals died of disease and supplies were cut off by the enemy.

When Henry invaded France in 1544, English soldiers guzzled their way through the countryside. They ate so much they caused a famine! Soldiers stole chickens and ducks, shot hares and drove pigs and sheep into their camp. Some men were especially cruel and cunning. They tied up a bull to make it bellow. When this brought the cows running they were swiftly turned into roast beef.

Naturally Henry himself never went hungry. Even in

a war he had 200 kitchen staff just to cook his meals. The King's meals-on-wheels included a bakehouse, a wine wagon, a buttery, a wagon for poultry, one for confectionery and a fresh food larder. These wagons had to be dragged through mud and rain just so that greedy Henry could have his supper. The kitchen staff all had weapons and had to be ready to use them.

Here for the beer
Henry's soldiers liked their beer. They liked it even more than food. A good supply of beer was essential to get any army on the move. Equally a beer shortage could bring a whole campaign to a halt.

A beer crisis first raised its frothy head in 1512. That year Henry sent troops to help the Spanish against the French. The English barmy army was stunned to find

beer wasn't being served. The sissy Spanish only drank wine and cider.

'No beer, no battle,' declared the English soldiers. A red-faced Henry had to bring them home. A year later Henry was preparing his army for France. This time brew-houses in Portsmouth were set up to make hundreds of tons of beer a day. But the soldiers grumbled the country beer wasn't as good as London ale. And when the London beer arrived it wasn't much better. 'Small as penny ale and as sour as crab,' moaned Admiral of the Fleet, Thomas Howard.

But beer did once help Henry to win a battle. It happened during his invasion of Scotland in 1542. The Duke of Norfolk was in charge of the English army. His dispatches to Henry with news of the war could have been something like this:

1/ Beer supply late arriving. Have had to delay invasion of Scotland by nine days.

2/ Good news – beer arrived at last. Bad news – beer ran dry after four days

3/ Fear mutiny from beer-thirsty troops. Have had to pull back across the border.

4/ Help! Scots pursuing us across the border. They think we're running away from them.

5/ Three cheers for the beer! Scots army bogged down in the marshes. Battle of Solway Moss a soggy walk-over. 20 Scots killed, hundreds drowned, 12,000 taken prisoner.

So the beer delayed the fight, the weather changed for the worse, and the sodden Scots suffered a complete washout.

MAKE MINE A PINT!

Blasted guns

Guns were the new fashion for armies in the 16th century. Bows were faster and more accurate, but every army had the new artillery as well. A Tudor gun wasn't much like the ones you see today. It was called an arquebus. The arquebus was supposed to be a handgun. Actually it was about as handy as a stone-age catapult. Firing it could be a risky business.

HOW TO FIRE AN ARQUEBUS

1 LOAD POWDER AND BALL CAREFULLY WHILE DODGING ENEMY FIRE.

2 RAISE THE GUN INTO FIRING POSITION.

3. LIGHT THE FUSE

4 BE CAREFUL YOUR GUN DOESN'T GET CLOGGED OR BROKEN...

5. OR RUINED BY THE RAIN...

6 IF YOU HAVE DIFFICULTIES CONSULT A GUNSMITH

Call a doctor! (On second thoughts. . .)

Henry's armies often suffered from disease. Diets were hardly healthy and infection spread easily in the camps. Two common complaints were measles and diarrhoea.

If you actually made it to the battlelines, a wound meant you were in the hands of the camp surgeons. These doctors were handy with sword or saw if you needed an arm or leg chopped off. Surgery was a frightening ordeal. The only anaesthetic was often a bottle of wine or brandy. After cutting your leg off the doctor would 'cauterize' the wound. This meant burning the flesh around the wound to stop infection spreading. Oddly enough, the survival rate for treatment wasn't very high.

Sponging mercenaries

Not all of Henry's army were fighting for their king. Some of them were fighting for cash. Professional soldiers called mercenaries were used by every army. They would fight for anyone who paid their wages. German soldiers were especially popular. But the trouble was they didn't get on with the English fighting on the same side. Fights often broke out before a battle had even started. Once a report reached the Duke of Norfolk that a German soldier had attacked an Englishman for no reason 'with a boar spear in the throat'. It sounded less than friendly. But Norfolk had no luck finding the culprit. His German friends swore blind they'd seen nothing.

Rotten weather

Bad weather could bring the mightiest of armies to its knees.

In 1523 the English were only 50 miles from Paris when the weather turned cold. It wasn't just a nippy French frost, it was more like the Arctic! In only two days 100 men froze to death. Those who lived watched their nails drop off with frostbite. At last the weather got warmer, but it hadn't finished its tricks. Next the rain poured down in torrents. The invading army was left to toil home in a sea of mud, starving and miserable. Back in England, it was a long time before any of the generals dared face Henry.

Henry's leaky navy

The English navy was founded by Henry VII. But it was his son who turned it into a fighting force. Henry VIII founded a guild responsible for:

> ...*the reformation of the navy, lately much decayed by the admission of young men without experience, and of Scots, Flemings and Frenchmen.*

(Naturally it was assumed all Englishmen made good sailors!)

It wasn't just the quality of the crew, the ships were in a bad way too. Henry set about building a bigger and better navy. By the end of his reign he had a fleet of 80 ships. The biggest of all was named *The Great Harry* (what else?). It weighed 1,000 tons and could carry 400 soldiers on top of its crew of 300. But one of Henry's most famous ships ended up at the bottom of Portsmouth harbour. It was a red-faced day for Henry. Here's how he might have described it.

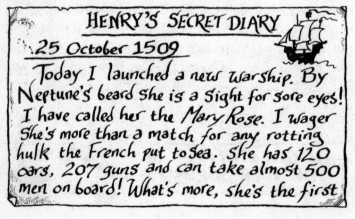

HENRY'S SECRET DIARY

25 October 1509

Today I launched a new warship. By Neptune's beard she is a sight for sore eyes! I have called her the *Mary Rose*. I wager she's more than a match for any rotting hulk the French put to sea. She has 120 oars, 207 guns and can take almost 500 men on board! What's more, she's the first to be fitted with heavy cannon on the broadside.

I passed these facts— and many more such details— to my sister Mary, as she launched the ship. She was much fascinated, though I fancy she tried to stifle a yawn after I'd talked for an hour or so.

'By the devil!' I roared in her ear. 'If the French ever dare to come near her the Mary Rose will blow them out of the water you wait and see!

19 JULY 1545

Failure! Disgrace! Misery! That leaking hulk the Mary Rose has made me look a fool in front of my friends and enemies. I was dining on board her today at Portsmouth when word came that the French fleet had been sighted.

The ruffians were coming to attack us! I left the Mary Rose and ordered the whole fleet to sail out and meet the enemy. I haven't felt so excited since I got rid of my last wife. 'What a surprise those French knaves will get,' I thought, 'when they see the Mary Rose bearing down on them.'

From our viewpoint we could see the smoke

and hear the thunder of cannon. Then the cowardly French turned tail and fled.

We watched the *Mary Rose* turn back towards the harbour. And that's when it happened. Her gun ports were still open. A gust of wind blew her over and she took in water. The ship suddenly capsized and sank like a stone. It happened so quickly, no one on board had time to escape. I'm told almost the entire crew of 500 drowned. The shame of it! I'll wager those knavish French are laughing all the way across the channel!

SNIGGER

HEE HEE!

Nobbling the nobles

One famous supporter of the war against France was the Duke of Buckingham.

Buckingham was the richest and most powerful noble in the land. Gossip said that if Henry died without a son, Buckingham would claim the crown. Henry always suspected people of plotting to pinch his crown. So it was only a matter of time before the finger pointed at Buckingham. The Duke was descended from Edward III and had plenty of supporters. But he had powerful enemies too. Among them was old big-head, Cardinal Wolsey. Henry asked his chief minister to keep an eye on Buckingham. Naturally the crafty cardinal did better than that.

FOR THE CHOP:

EDWARD STAFFORD, DUKE OF BUCKINGHAM.

*How I'd love to get my hands on that Wolsey!
That snake in the grass! That prattling parrot! He
was always jealous of me. Just because I was of
royal blood and not a butcher's boy like him. He
hung around Henry like poison in the air, waiting
his chance. A gentleman would have challenged me
to a duel. But not Wolsey, that cowardly cur. He
went sneaking behind my back, digging up dirt. He
bribed my own servants to tell lies about me. They
were all in it together – my surveyor (a knave), my
confessor (a vile villain), and my chaplain (a two-
faced traitor). Just listen to the foul accusations
they made:*

*1 I often cursed Wolsey's name out loud. (Lies!
Lies! May he roast in hell!)*

*2 I was sorry I'd missed my chance to cut off the
Cardinal's fat head when the King was ill.*

*3 I had consulted a star-gazing monk who told me
that one day I would be king.*

*4 I was (mark this!) plotting to murder the King.
My plan (they claim) was to approach the King*

with a knife hidden in my cloak and stab him to death. (A plan so marvellous 'clever' only a fool like Wolsey could have thought of it!) I vowed my innocence to the King but my words fell on deaf ears.

I see how the land lies now. I'm rich, I'm loved by all, I've got royal blood and powerful friends. Henry wanted me out of the way so he got that viper Wolsey to arrange it.

I was tried before the House of Lords. Half of them were my own relatives! But it didn't stop them finding me guilty. They were too busy saving their own scrawny necks to care about mine.

500 soldiers guarded the scaffold as I went up for my execution. Even to the bitter end Henry was scared of me. He was worried the London mob might come to my rescue. Our noble king didn't even come to watch his old friend die. They said he was in bed with a fever. I pray God it was serious.

As I lay my head on the block, men and women wept aloud. It took three strokes of the axe to chop off my head. I always was a tough old bird.

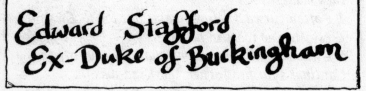

Edward Stafford
Ex-Duke of Buckingham

When Buckingham got the chop Henry lost one of his oldest friends. One of the next to go was his second wife.

The Tudor Tatler

20 May 1536

HENRY DITCHES 'THE WITCH'

Anne Boleyn is dead. Only four months after the King buried his first wife he has now seen off his second, *writes rogue reporter Ralph Quill*.

To lose one wife is unfortunate, to lose two begins to look like carelessness. This king goes too far says *The Tudor Tatler*. It's time he started listening to his subjects.

Under a spell

Anne Boleyn was not everyone's pin-up queen. Some said it was a scandal that Henry ever married her. 'She was a scheming minx, just one of Catherine's ladies-in-waiting till the King clapped his greedy eyes on her,' said a courtier – who prefers not to

be named. Others went further. They claim Anne was secretly a witch. Now this paper can reveal the evidence. Study this recent picture of the Queen.

claims, 'Anne did cast a spell over me from the moment we met. She was mistress of the black arts of witchcraft.' But Henry would say that. He wanted any excuse to get rid of

Happy crowds at Anne's coronation

her. He sang a different tune in the beginning when he was in love. His secret love letters (published tomorrow only in *The Tudor Tatler*) are full of passion:

'I would you were in mine arms or I in yours, for I think it is a long time since we kissed'

writes smitten Henry. No mention of witchcraft there!

Henry was hoping for a quick divorce so he'd have young Anne in his arms. But Queen Catherine soon put a damper on that. It took seven years before Anne got her wedding day. Even then, we can reveal, the service was held in secret because Henry's divorce hadn't come through. For a short while our noble king was married to two different wives!

No cheers for the queen

Anne must have dreamed of her coronation as her finest hour. In fact it was a shambles. As she rode through the packed streets of London, there was an eerie silence. No one cheered or waved their hats. Nobody cried out 'God save the Queen.'

'The city is well enough,' grumbled Anne, *'but I saw so many caps on heads and heard*

but few tongues.'

To her subjects, Anne would always be the king's mistress. They called her 'goggle eyes' and common 'Nan Bullen'. In their view she wasn't fit to wipe the dainty Spanish boots of Catherine.

Even the coronation itself was a nightmare. Poor Anne was heavily pregnant and needed to go to the loo frequently. She couldn't leave the church during the long ceremony so two of her ladies had to sit under her table. Their job was to be ready with a chamber pot when Anne needed it. What a relief when it was all over!

Boy trouble

Witch or not, Anne's spell over Henry didn't last long. Within three years he was tired of her. All the court doctors and star-gazers had predicted her baby would be a boy. The names had even been chosen, Henry or Edward. But when the child came it was a girl.

Elizabeth

Anne tried again but she lost the baby. Henry, meanwhile, lost his patience. He accused Anne of having other boyfriends. One of them, we can reveal, was court dancer, Mark Smeaton. Smeaton was arrested and soon confessed.

(He was being stretched on the rack at the time so you can't blame him.) From that hour, no magic could save Anne. She was accused of treason which meant Henry wanted the death penalty. Unlike Catherine of Aragon, Anne had no powerful connections to protect her. She was taken by boat to the Tower of London.

'She fell at my feet weeping,' the Constable of the Tower told our reporter. 'She didn't strike me as a happy person.'

Early on the 19 May Anne was executed. Not on Tower Hill as usual but inside the Tower on the Green. Why the break with tradition? *The Tudor Tatler* can reveal our noble king was scared. He was worried what Anne might say before she died. He needn't have bothered his big head. Anne died with dignity. Her last words were, '*May Jesus Christ save my sovereign master the King, the most godly, noble and gentle Prince that is, and long to reign over you.*'

She knelt down at the block. She carefully tucked her long black hair under a cap to bare her neck. Then she was blindfolded. The executioner, an expert swordsman, had come from France at Anne's request. He stepped forward and cut off her head with one blow. It was so quick, people said Anne's lips were still moving in prayer afterwards.

Anne didn't even have the comfort of dying a queen.

Henry – that 'most godly, noble and gentle Prince' – had got a divorce just before the execution.

THE TATLER COMMENT

Was this woman a witch who deserved to die? This paper says 'Not guilty.' Any guilt lies with our cruel-hearted king. 'The wife swapping must stop here, Henry!' says *The Tudor Tatler*. 'Or else England might decide it's time to swap the king!'

ARTY HENRY

A song, a dance and a chicken drumstick

By the mid-1530s fashions were changing. So was Henry's waistline. It was growing bigger. And bigger. Not that anyone dared to say he was fat or anything...

WHO SAID **FAT?**

No, he was just well rounded. And big as he was, he was always the height of fashion – which was more than you could say for the other Henrys before him. Take a look at the history of Henry's fashion.

HENRY V – A SOLDIER

HENRY VI – A TRAMP.

HENRY VII – THE CHEAP AND BORING LOOK.

HENRY VIII - KING OF THE CATWALK

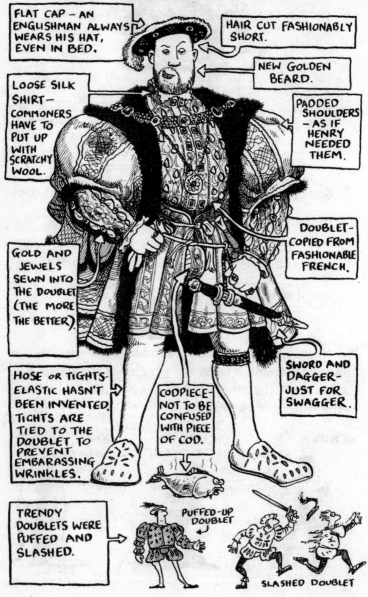

FLAT CAP - AN ENGLISHMAN ALWAYS WEARS HIS HAT, EVEN IN BED.

HAIR CUT FASHIONABLY SHORT.

NEW GOLDEN BEARD.

LOOSE SILK SHIRT — COMMONERS HAVE TO PUT UP WITH SCRATCHY WOOL.

PADDED SHOULDERS – AS IF HENRY NEEDED THEM.

DOUBLET — COPIED FROM FASHIONABLE FRENCH.

GOLD AND JEWELS SEWN INTO THE DOUBLET (THE MORE THE BETTER).

HOSE OR TIGHTS — ELASTIC HASN'T BEEN INVENTED. TIGHTS ARE TIED TO THE DOUBLET TO PREVENT EMBARASSING WRINKLES.

CODPIECE — NOT TO BE CONFUSED WITH PIECE OF COD.

SWORD AND DAGGER — JUST FOR SWAGGER.

TRENDY DOUBLETS WERE PUFFED AND SLASHED.

PUFFED-UP DOUBLET

SLASHED DOUBLET

Henry's girls

Most foreigners agreed that English women were badly dressed. But then, as Henry would have said:

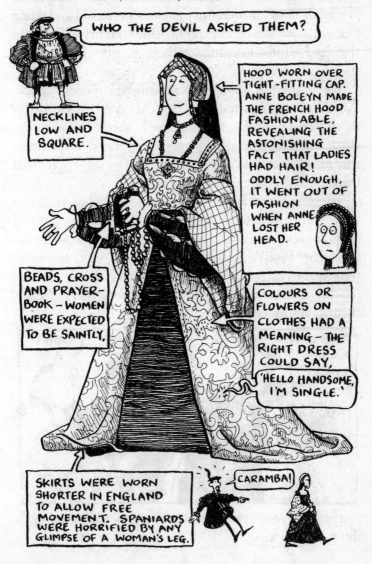

WHO THE DEVIL ASKED THEM?

NECKLINES LOW AND SQUARE.

HOOD WORN OVER TIGHT-FITTING CAP. ANNE BOLEYN MADE THE FRENCH HOOD FASHIONABLE, REVEALING THE ASTONISHING FACT THAT LADIES HAD HAIR! ODDLY ENOUGH, IT WENT OUT OF FASHION WHEN ANNE LOST HER HEAD.

BEADS, CROSS AND PRAYER-BOOK – WOMEN WERE EXPECTED TO BE SAINTLY.

COLOURS OR FLOWERS ON CLOTHES HAD A MEANING – THE RIGHT DRESS COULD SAY, 'HELLO HANDSOME, I'M SINGLE.'

SKIRTS WERE WORN SHORTER IN ENGLAND TO ALLOW FREE MOVEMENT. SPANIARDS WERE HORRIFIED BY ANY GLIMPSE OF A WOMAN'S LEG.

CARAMBA!

Henry's glittering court

Henry wanted his court to be the envy of Europe. He set out to bring the best musicians, writers and painters to England. Sixteenth-century palaces were cold and damp places (there was no central heating). Henry warmed up the cold winter evenings with banquets, dancing and spectacular shows.

Top of the bill was an entertainment called a *masque*. A masque wasn't something to wear on your face. It was more like a pantomime without the jokes. It had songs, music, dancing and breathtaking scenery. Sometimes the masque-makers built entire castles or enchanted forests and hid the performers inside.

The King and his court played all the parts. They were also the audience so they were sure to get a warm round of applause at the end. Dancers often wore masks (the other kind) to hide their identity. Henry's favourite trick was to disguise himself to fool his courtiers. In fact he did this so often that his courtiers had to train themselves to look amazed.

A typical evening at Henry's court would serve up a show fit for a king.

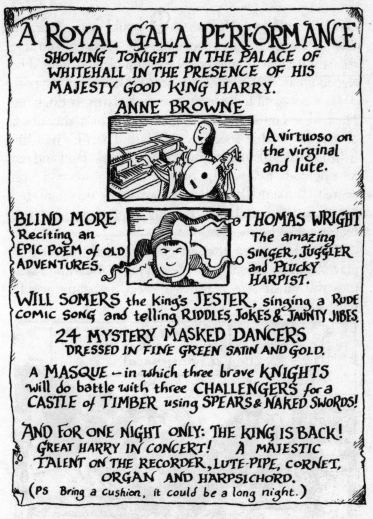

A ROYAL GALA PERFORMANCE

SHOWING TONIGHT IN THE PALACE OF
WHITEHALL IN THE PRESENCE OF HIS
MAJESTY GOOD KING HARRY.

ANNE BROWNE

A virtuoso on the virginal and lute.

BLIND MORE Reciting an EPIC POEM of OLD ADVENTURES.

THOMAS WRIGHT The amazing SINGER, JUGGLER and PLUCKY HARPIST.

WILL SOMERS the king's JESTER, singing a RUDE COMIC SONG and telling RIDDLES, JOKES & JAUNTY JIBES.

24 MYSTERY MASKED DANCERS
DRESSED IN FINE GREEN SATIN AND GOLD.

A MASQUE — in which three brave KNIGHTS will do battle with three CHALLENGERS for a CASTLE of TIMBER using SPEARS & NAKED SWORDS!

AND FOR ONE NIGHT ONLY: THE KING IS BACK! GREAT HARRY IN CONCERT! A MAJESTIC TALENT ON THE RECORDER, LUTE-PIPE, CORNET, ORGAN AND HARPSICHORD.
(PS Bring a cushion, it could be a long night.)

The tragic tale of the miffed minstrel

The fame of Henry's court spread far and wide. Musicians, acrobats and storytellers all over Europe heard that England was the place to make their fortune. In Venice a musician called Zuam da Leze hit the glory trail. He was certain a man of Henry's taste would appreciate his talents. Da Leze was a wizard of the clavicembalo. He thought if Henry could only hear him play once, he'd be signed up as a court musician on a fat salary.

Da Leze gambled everything on his trip to England. He had a craftsman in Venice make him the finest clavicembalo that money could buy. Then he had the instrument carted thousands of miles across land and sea to England. Every step of the way he worried and fretted. What if the delicate instrument was damaged before he had a chance to play it? But da Leze was lucky – or so he thought.

When he arrived at court Henry agreed to hear him play. Zuam da Leze began. He put all his heart and soul into the music. He played so sweetly a statue would have wept.

At the end the King clapped and got up to go. Puzzled, da Leze waited to be begged to stay on at court. Instead a servant appeared, handed him a purse of 20 nobles (about £7.00) and thanked him politely for his performance.

Zuam da Leze was stunned. Was that it? The money wouldn't even cover what he'd paid for the instrument! He was ruined. Broke. And worse, he was stuck in England without a job.

Over dinner he sank into despair. Around him Henry's nobles guzzled their beef and slurped their wine. What did they care if glum Zuam's life was ruined?

Da Leze took a knife from his belt. While no one was paying any attention, he plunged it into his own chest.

Servants saw the blood. They quickly carried the visitor off to a nearby bedroom. They didn't want the King put off his supper by a miserable dying minstrel!

The servants calmed da Leze down and bandaged his wound. But the musician had decided he'd played his last movement. When they left him alone, he hanged himself by his own belt.

No one knew what became of the unlucky clavicembalo. Maybe Henry kept if for himself.

NICE TONE, 'TIS PITY ABOUT THE BLOOD...

'May I have this dance?'

There's no doubt Henry was a mover and a groover in his day. He sometimes danced till dawn, showing no sign of getting tired. The Italian ambassador once watched Henry go straight from jousting practice in the tilt-yard to frolicking on the dance floor.

> *He does wonders and leaps like a stag. He was fresher after this awful exertion than before. I do not know how he can stand it.*

The dances that Henry and his court did weren't like today's. You couldn't just get on the floor and do your own thing. Henry had spent hours in his youth practising the moves. He had to dip, hop and bow in just the right places.

Three famous dances of the time were called the pavane, the galliard and the volta. The pavane was so slow scholars could dance it in their long gowns without tripping up and making a dunce of themselves. The galliard was quicker and the volta was hot stuff. Henry would grab his partner round the waist and actually lift her into the air. (A good job it wasn't the other way around!) Gentlemen were advised to remove their swords for the volta; it could lead to nasty accidents.

Meanwhile, Henry went on changing partners. No sooner did the cannon fire to announce Anne Boleyn's death, than Henry galloped off to see his new girlfriend. Her name was Jane Seymour. Unfortunately for her, she didn't last long either.

WE INTERRUPT THIS CHAPTER TO BRING YOU TRAGIC NEWS...

The Tudor Tatler

25 October 1537

PLAIN JANE IN SHOCK DEATH

Queen Jane gone but not forgotten

Queen Jane Seymour died shortly before midnight last night, *writes rogue reporter, Ralph Quill.*

Poor Jane lasted only 18 months on the throne. King Henry is said to be heartbroken. What a year it has been for the 46-year-old king! Only 12 days ago he was the happiest man alive. At last he had a royal son. It had taken Henry 30 years of marriage and three wives to achieve his dream. But last night it all went wrong.

The King looked pale and drawn this morning as he

111

spoke of his grief.

'*Divine Providence,*' he said, '*has mingled my joy with the bitterness of the death of her who brought me this happiness.*'

No wild child

The Tudor Tatler joins the nation in mourning today. People are calling the Queen '*the most virtuous lady that ever lived*'. Where Anne Boleyn was wild and bewitching, Plain Jane was sweet and sensible.

She rose to fame the usual way – charming the King behind the Queen's back. Anne Boleyn was Catherine's lady-in-waiting. Jane was Anne Boleyn's. No prizes for guessing Jane's first act as queen. She made sure her maids kept out of the limelight! One of them, attractive Anne Basset, recalled, 'I was told my French gown would not be suitable. The truth was the Queen didn't want me catching the King's eye.'

Anne Bassett – dressed by the Queen

Scratch and tiff

Jane herself was no pin-up queen. Maybe Henry chose her because he wanted peace and quiet after his stormy marriage to Anne Boleyn. There were rumours of talons bared between Anne and Jane. But Jane was no bare-faced flirt. Henry once sent her a present of gold sovereigns with the message that people were making up rude ballads about them. Shocked Jane sent the money right back and begged the King to consider her reputation.

Nevertheless, Jane didn't hang back when she saw her chance. *The Tatler* can reveal

Henry and Jane opt for quickie wedding

that only 24 hours after Anne's head rolled off the block, Jane was secretly engaged to the King. The marriage took place just ten days later in the Queen's rooms. Pity there wasn't time to take Anne's coat of arms off the walls.

But Henry was happy with his sensible, plain Jane.

Happy family

At home she played the role of palace peacemaker. It was her influence that restored daughter Mary to her dad's favour. Mary had been in disgrace since her mother, Catherine of Aragon, was sent from court. Jane knew better than to get in Henry's bad books, though. Only once did she make the mistake of arguing with him. Henry's pointed remark about '*the last queen's meddling*' soon shut her up!

Boy, oh joy

Then, on 12 Oct 1537, Jane achieved what Catherine and Anne never could. She gave

Room for one more? The royal chapel at Windsor

birth to a healthy baby boy, Edward. Court insiders claim the King wept like a child as he held the boy in his arms. Bonfires were lit around the country, 2,000 cannon fired from the Tower of London and the bells rang out in every church. Only 12 days later the same churches were draped in funeral black. Jane had caught a fever at the birth and never recovered. She was buried in the chapel at Windsor. The King vowed to join his favourite wife there one day.

THE TATLER COMMENT

You can't help but feel sorry for sad old Henry. He gets rid of two wives who don't please him and what happens? He finds one he's fond of and she ups and dies. Fate can be hard even on cruel kings.

Perhaps after three wives Henry's had a bellyful of married life?

We say 'Don't count on it'. The rumour is that he's already hunting for wife no. 4, 'for the

sake of the realm'. Pull the other one, Your Royal Highness! For the sake of Henry, more like.

Manners maketh monarchs

All Henry's wives would have been taught good manners as part of their upbringing. Manners were important in Tudor times. It wasn't just a matter of being polite. Correct behaviour was a mark of nobility. You wouldn't last long at Henry's court if you didn't know whether to burp or hold your wind after a hearty supper.

Test your own Tudor manners. Can you tell which of these are manners that would impress Henry and which might get him sharpening that axe?

Good manners?

1 Always greet a woman with a kiss.

2 Always greet a man with a kiss.

3 Wipe your nose on the tablecloth at meals.

4 Check what's in your hanky after blowing your nose.

5 Spit on the floor and tread it into the carpet.

6 Burp loudly to show you're a lover of good food.

7 Fart loudly to show you're a lover of good food.

8 Clean your teeth with a toothpick after eating.

9 Wear fur next to your skin to attract fleas.

10 Sleep with your mouth open and a hole in your nightcap.

Answers:

1 Good manners – the Dutch scholar Erasmus complained that when he visited an English house he had to kiss everyone, including the cat!

2 Good manners – Henry kissed his pals on the cheek.

3 Bad manners – Tudor advice on good behaviour said: 'wipe your nose with a hanky – not on your gown or the tablecloth'. Only commoners used their sleeves, probably because they didn't own a hanky in the first place.

4 Bad manners – never examine your bogies in public, thank you.

5 Good manners – spitting on the floor was accepted. It was polite to tread spit into the rushes covering the floor. But spitting in someone's face was a sign of contempt.

6 Good manners – burping wasn't rude (again, unless you did it in your neighbour's face).

7 Bad manners – only drunks and idiots broke wind at dinner. Kindly take your smells downwind.

8 Good manners – pick away! Toothpicks were the Tudor toothbrush.

9 Good manners – yes, even Henry had fleas. He wore a piece of fur under his shirt to attract them all to one place.

10 Good manners – sleeping with your mouth open was meant to keep your breath sweet. People were advised to wear a red nightcap with a hole in it 'through which the vapour may go out'.

The dinner club

We mentioned Henry's, ahem, expanding waistline. Was a fat belly frowned upon in Tudor times? Some writers did warn against overeating but that's because Henry wasn't alone in being a porker. Eating was a national hobby for the English nobility. If there had been a World Guzzling Championship the English would have won it hands down and bottoms up. Meals went on for hours, punctuated by burps going off like cannon all round the table. Some people got worried about the length of meals in the 16th century. People were spending so long at table they didn't have time for much else! Henry loved his food more than most – as his diary might have shown.

HENRY'S SECRET DIARY

It's been a full day. Come to think of it, I'm pretty full as well. After a spot of tennis this morning (beat Suffolk again, ha!) found I'd worked up quite a hunger. Had a thumping great lunch, then went hawking in the forest. A warm summer's day.

By the time we got back I was looking forward mightily to supper. The Emperor's ambassador dined with me, so ordered a goodly spread and we all got stuck in. By my oath! I was as stuffed as a Christmas turkey by the finish! Could hardly move.

R. PEACOCK. V. TASTY!   MMM! PRAWNS!

We sat down to eat at seven in the evening and rose seven hours later at two in the morning. Well you can't hurry supper!

As well as beef, mutton, pork, rabbit, peacock and the usual meats I ordered the cook to make my favourite prawn pasties. We had twenty different kinds marvellously baked in the shape of castles, stags, boars and fish. I swear as each new dish was brought in on a silver platter the ambassador's eyes were nearly popping out of his head.

R CASTLE! YUMMY!

We washed it all down with the finest French and German wines, followed by sweet honey and spiced wines.

Urp! That's better. Settling down for the night in my room now with my bedtime drink — a hot mug of sugared ale laced with hot milk, eggs and grated biscuit.

Mmmm. Sumptuous!

Wonder what's for breakfast tomorrow? Am feeling a bit peckish...

Henry's mates

Whatever Henry did – eating, hunting or gambling – he liked to do it with his pals. Courtiers were there to keep Henry company. If the King wanted to play cards, they wanted to play cards too. If he wanted a race, they ordered their horses to be saddled. Henry liked fun and games. If there was nothing to do, he got bored and threw sugar plums at his guests to keep himself amused.

Henry's pals were men like himself. Big, hearty, sporty types who were handy in a joust or a battle. But Henry had an arty, intellectual side to him too. He liked his court to be a magnet for famous artists and scholars.

Give them a Harry

Today's celebs are rock and film stars, but the megastars of Tudor times were writers, painters and thinkers. Henry probably would have enjoyed the Oscars ceremony in Hollywood every year. He loved any chance to dress up and show off. So what if he'd held his own Tudor version of the Oscars? Who would have been making the thank you speeches?

THE HARRY FOR BEST POET GOES TO...

Thomas Wyatt

Who's he?

One of Henry's most celebrated courtiers and poets. All courtiers were supposed to write poetry but Wyatt was the real thing – a bard with blue blood.

Claim to fame?
King of lurve poetry. If you fancied someone at court you had to follow the strict rules of courtly love. Lovers were supposed to:
a) Wear their lady's favour when jousting. (This could be a ribbon or something in her colours.)
b) Send her a gift on Valentine's Day.
c) Write her mushy love poems.
The last one was a problem. Many courtiers couldn't write a poem to charm a pig. They solved the problem by paying professional poets to write love poems for them. Wyatt himself didn't need any help, he had poems coming out of his ears. They were addressed to lots of different women – which didn't mean he fell in love every Tuesday. Wyatt was just doing his job.

Worst career move?
Writing a poem to Anne Boleyn around the time Henry had her in his sights. The poem contained these words as if spoken by Anne: 'Noli me tangere for Caesar's I am/And wild for to hold although I seem tame.' Roughly translated it meant, 'Hands off buster, I'm the king's babe.' Since Wyatt was always writing love poems to beautiful women, he got away with it. But only just. When Anne was arrested, Wyatt was also made a guest in the Tower of London. (He was rumoured to be one of Anne's ex-boyfriends.) The plucky poet kept mum about the romance and soon after Henry pardoned him.

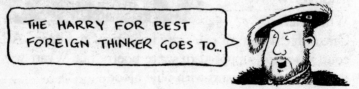

THE HARRY FOR BEST FOREIGN THINKER GOES TO...

Erasmus

Er . . . who?

You know, we met him earlier.

Remind me.

A great scholar and thinker, Erasmus was a Dutchman living in Italy. He hated the thought of the long sea journey to England (he got seasick). So what did he do? He hopped on a boat and came to England where he stayed for five years. Pretty dumb for a great thinker! But Erasmus had heard so much about the young and brilliant Henry, he was dying to meet him for himself.

Claim to fame?

Big name humanist. Humanists like Erasmus and Thomas More studied the classical writings of the ancients – Greek writers like Plato and Homer.

Worst prediction?

In 1519 Erasmus said he had found 'a model of Christian society'. He was referring to the court of King Henry VIII. Daft as it sounds, Erasmus reckoned Henry was the most moral king he'd ever met. You have to remember this was in the early years of Henry's reign. By the time the chopping block was in regular action, Erasmus had packed his bags and gone home. Well, even great thinkers can make a mistake.

John Heywood

Another great thinker?

No, a passable playwright. Early Tudor plays were either

mystery plays based on the Bible or morality plays which warned people to lead a good life. It was all serious stuff. Only in Henry VIII's reign did the idea of comedy catch on. Heywood was the man who made England laugh.

Claim to fame?

Wrote plays for nearly 70 years from the 1520s to shortly before he died in 1587. They're known as Tudor Interludes. Heywood also made his living as one of Henry's minstrels and then as court jester to Edward VI and Mary. A play, a song, a joke – he was a John of all trades.

Worst career move?

Not changing his name to William Shakespeare. Marlowe, Jonson and Shakespeare were the stars of the great Elizabethan age of drama. Sadly Heywood just missed it. He died five years before Shakespeare's first play was performed.

THE HARRY FOR BEST FOREIGN FLATTERER GOES TO...

Hans Holbein the Younger

Hans who?

An artist and not just any artist. Holbein was Henry's court painter. He arrived in 1526 from Switzerland and settled at the English court.

Why Holbein the Younger? Didn't he get old?

Yes, but his dad was also a painter called Hans Holbein. When Holbein Senior had a son he modestly decided to name the boy after himself. The son was known as Holbein the Younger to avoid mix-ups.

Claim to fame?

Painting portraits. Henry banned all religious images as 'popish' Catholicism. So people were the safest thing to paint. Holbein painted all the rich and famous at Henry's court leaving us marvellous records of what they looked like. Most of them are still kept at Windsor Castle. Top court servants like Henry's astronomer and falconer modelled for Holbein. Henry also employed him to paint the women he fancied as future brides. It wasn't done for a king to go and inspect the goods himself, so Henry sent Holbein to paint a portrait and bring it back. After Jane Seymour's death, Holbein had a particularly busy year. He travelled Europe painting every woman that Henry had heard was rich and good looking. Unfortunately for Holbein, the one that caught Henry's eye was the picture of Anne of Cleves.

Worst career move?

Painting Anne of Cleves. Henry loved the portrait and decided to marry Anne on the strength of it. But Holbein's picture turned out to be much better-looking than Anne.

Henry who?
Thou jesteth!
Claim to fame?
King of England.
Besides that, stupid?

As we know, Henry was a mean musician, a princely poet and no slouch at songwriting. 'Greensleeves' is his best known hit. Or it would have been, if he'd written it. Sadly, experts doubt it was one of Henry's ditties.

Henry's other famous song was 'Pastime with Good Company'. Not such a catchy title, but still a big hit in its day. The King's songs weren't only popular in court, you could hear them sung in inns and alehouses (where 'Closing Time with Pickled Company' was a favourite).

Some of Henry's lyrics weren't exactly Shakespeare. Here's a sample:

> *The daisy delectable*
> *The violet wan and blue,*
> *Ye are not more variable*
> *I love you and no more.*

Pity about Greensleeves really.
Best career move?
Not giving up the day job.

The Tudor Tatler

9 July 1540

HENRY TURNS NAG OUT TO GRAZE

by rogue reporter Ralph Quill.

Holbein's portrait   *The real Anne of Cleves*

Talk about a royal disaster! Fed-up Henry VIII has ended his latest marriage after only six months. The King was persuaded to marry 23-year-old Anne of Cleves after seeing her portrait. But now Henry claims the marriage should never have got under starter's orders. The reason? He thinks his bride is as ugly as a horse!

Dud match

The man blamed for not putting the King in the picture is Chancellor Thomas Cromwell. He suggested the match and has plenty of time to regret it now. He's in the Tower waiting to be executed. Lawyers say he'll only live long enough to give evidence in the King's latest divorce case.

Cromwell to blame

Cromwell's envoy was Nicholas Wotton. Wotton went on a mission last year to inspect the Duke of Cleves's daughters. It was a delicate business, he told *The Tatler*. 'The daughters were shown to us but they were so wrapped up we could see neither their figures nor their faces. When I protested, the German chancellor lost his temper. "Why?" he bellowed. "Do you want to see them naked?"'

Hans Holbein, the famous court painter, was the next to pack his easel for Germany. He painted Anne's picture for Henry to see for himself. '*I thought he expressed their images very lively*,' said Wotton. Too lively as it turns out! Henry was so taken with the picture that the marriage was quickly arranged.

Sneak preview

Anne didn't come to England until after Christmas. Even then she stayed in Rochester on her way to London. But hot-blooded Henry was too impatient to wait any longer. The King planned to disguise himself and sneak a look at his new bride. It would be his New Year surprise for Anne. As it turned out it was Henry who got the surprise!

His Majesty's cunning disguise

The King arrived dressed in a hooded cloak. First he sent Master of the Horse, Sir Anthony Browne, to announce the delivery of his New Year's gift. Sir Anthony has never forgotten that embarrassing day. He told *The Tatler* the full story:

'Lady Anne was watching the bull-baiting from her window when the King came up the stairs. Henry didn't wait for introductions. He rushed straight up and planted a kiss on her. The poor girl blushed to her fingertips. She stammered a few words in German. Then she went back to staring out of the window.

'In truth it was an awkward moment. She obviously hadn't a clue who her hooded visitor was. And to make matters worse she couldn't speak a word of English.

The delighted king meets his new bride

'Henry meanwhile looked as if he'd seen a ghost. You'd have thought Anne was the ugliest witch on earth! There was nothing for it but for Henry to beat a red-faced retreat.'

Sew, sew

Henry's opinion of his new bride was summed up in four words. '*I like her not*,' he told Cromwell.

Court gossip says Anne was never cut out to be an English queen. Friends say her hobbies are needlework and talking to her mother. German ladies it turns out aren't expected to read books or learn music. Anne's singing could clear a room in ten seconds.

Given her upbringing, the marriage was doomed from the start. After six months, it's no great surprise that Henry's gone roving again. This time it's little Catherine Howard who has caught his eye. As for Anne, she's been shipped out to Richmond and informed the King wants a divorce. If she goes quietly she's been promised an 'honoured position'. *The Tatler* can reveal her new title will be 'the King's sister'. (Only Henry has the nerve to turn his ex-wives into his sisters!)

Anne's response to the divorce is, '*that she is content always with Your Majesty.*' It may be the wisest thing she's ever said. Remember what happened to the last Anne to fall out with Henry?

THE TATLER COMMENT

Hard luck Henry! Wife number four was the biggest disaster of the lot. We doubt you'll be keeping Holbein's portrait by your bedside! But what about Anne herself? How did she feel about the marriage? She was marrying a man twice her age and probably three times her size. The King is old, unsteady on his legs, and as bad-tempered as a caged bear. He's certainly no oil painting himself.

We say, 'You're well out of it, Anne. Who wants to be a bewitching beauty like Anne Boleyn anyway? Better an ugly head than no head at all!'

Anne Boleyn - headless

Anne of Cleves - Henryless

TIMELINE:
THE ROTTEN YEARS.

1536-9 HENRY HAS A SMASHING TIME WITH THE MONASTERIES.

YOU'VE BEEN REFORMED

1540: HELLO WIFE NO.4, ANNE OF CLEVES. THOMAS CROMWELL GETS THE CHOP. HELLO NO.5, CATHERINE HOWARD.

EURGH!

PHWOAR!

1542: CATHERINE HOWARD JOINS THE CHOPPING LIST. BATTLE OF SOLWAY MOSS — SCOTS GET THAT SINKING FEELING.

IT'S A SOLWAY MESS!

SWIM FOR IT!

1543: COME IN NO.6 — CATHERINE PARR.

1547: COME IN HENRY — YOUR TIME IS UP!

URK

HOOLIGAN HENRY

Monks, magic and rebellions

By the 1530s, Henry started to notice an unfamiliar problem. The royal coffers were getting short of cash. His dad – Henry VII – had never been short of a crown or two. But then, dad was a miser. His palace at Richmond was known to locals as 'Rich Mount'. Once a gold coin went into Henry VII's strongbox, it never came out again. Henry VIII was the opposite. 'Spend, spend, spend,' was his motto. Henry's favourite colour was gold. His caps and doublets were gold, his buttons were gold, his sleeves were embroidered with gold. He made King Midas look like a beggar. On top of spending a fortune on clothes, he gambled away hundreds of pounds and spent millions on his wars. His piggy bank was bound to run dry sooner or later.

When Henry looked around for a way to make money, his eye fell on the monasteries. He was now Head of the Church and the Church was rich. The monasteries were stuffed with silver and gold plate. All that Henry needed was an excuse to get his hands on all that loot!

Step forward Thomas Cromwell. (Remember the last of the four Toms?) Cromwell was a tough nut, a hard-headed ex-soldier. Just the man for the job. Henry set him to work in 1535 to report on the size of the Church's piggy bank. But what he really wanted was an excuse to close them down.

On the face of it Cromwell's job looked a tough one.

How do you dig the dirt on a bunch of monks and nuns? Monks were the only people in England who did what all Christians were supposed to do. They went to Mass (church service) *eight* times a day. It didn't leave them much time to get up to any monkey business.

St Baldpate's Abbey
TODAY'S TIMETABLE

Dawn — Get up. Dress in hairy habits. Lauds (church service).

6 a.m. — Prime (church service)

7 a.m. — Breakfast – fish.

8 a.m. — Work duties – study and cleaning

9 a.m. — Chapter Mass (church service)

10 a.m. — Meeting with Abbot. Be on time please.

11 a.m. — High Mass (church service)

12 noon — Dinner – fish pie.

1 p.m. — Rest in dormitory.

2 p.m. — Work in monastery garden.

3 p.m. — Nones (church service).

4 p.m. — Back to work.

6 p.m. — Supper – boiled fish, you lucky monks

7 p.m. — Vespers (church service).

9 p.m. — Compline (church service).

10 p.m. — Lights out. No reading prayer-books under the covers.

Midnight: Get up you lazy layabouts! Time for Matins!

1 pm. — Sleep till dawn.

Have a nice day
The Abbot

LET US PRAY FOR CHIPS AND KETCHUP

You might think that Cromwell's report would have been pretty boring. That's where you'd be wrong! Monks in Tudor times had a bad reputation – and with some reason. While many of them got on with their studies and prayers, a few behaved in a very unholy manner. Comic ballads at the time were full of drunken monks and naughty nuns getting up to mischief.

Of course the popular stories were probably exaggerated. But Cromwell and his team didn't mind that. They could exaggerate as well as anyone! Henry sent them to find out if the monasteries were corrupt. They knew the answer he wanted to hear.

The news that came back to Henry had him rubbing his hands with glee.

With the facts we know, it's easy to imagine how the report might have looked.

Report of the Royal Commission.

To his majesty King Henry VIII, Supreme Head of the Church in England.

We, your loyal commissioners, are shocked! We visited the monasteries and convents throughout your kingdom.

We found them in a disgusting state. But that's nothing to the way the monks and nuns behave! We can't begin to tell Your Majesty the stories of foul indecency. But we'll do our best.

1. At the Benedictine Priory of Wymondham, the vestments worn for mass were in rags and tatters. The bread and wine was so mouldy and sour, a pig would have refused communion.

Yuk!

2. The monks of Westacre claim to be poor as church mice (if you can believe that!). They sold their most famous relic - a piece of St Andrew's finger - to pay for food to fill their greedy bellies.

fig. 1.
St Andrew's Finger - SOLD

fig. 2.
Fish Fingers - BOUGHT

3. A poor monk wrote to us begging to be set free. He says he's been in 'prison' since he was 13 years old. What foul dungeon did he mean? The monastery at Wynchelcombe! He claims his fellow brothers are as savage as wolves.

He begs to go back to the outside world to get away from the daily backbiting and brawls.

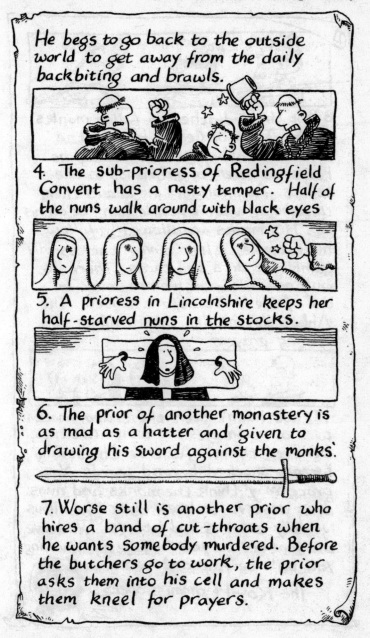

4. The sub-prioress of Redingfield Convent has a nasty temper. Half of the nuns walk around with black eyes

5. A prioress in Lincolnshire keeps her half-starved nuns in the stocks.

6. The prior of another monastery is as mad as a hatter and 'given to drawing his sword against the monks'.

7. Worse still is another prior who hires a band of cut-throats when he wants somebody murdered. Before the butchers go to work, the prior asks them into his cell and makes them kneel for prayers.

8 But the Godfather of fallen monks is the Abbot of Cerne. He lets the lands and abbey go hang while he keeps his harem of girlfriends in the cellars. At mealtimes he allows them to come up and sit beside him – or on his lap. His monks are allowed to follow his example. After dinner they usually gamble at dice and cards. There is only one rule – all women must be out of the house before sunset. The Abbot doesn't like them holding up evening prayers.

If we hadn't seen these abominations with our own eyes we would not have believed them. As true Christians we are shocked beyond words. Your grace may think the monks and nuns don't deserve to keep their marvellous wealthy estates and abbeys. We leave the matter to your Majesty, knowing you will be fair and wise.

The Royal Commissioners

Of course the report was full of whopping lies. For instance, the prior of Folkestone was reported as 'lazy'. In fact, when the visit took place he was busy repairing his own house (at his own expense), rebuilding the bakehouse and the monks' sleeping quarters. Idle sponger! Henry wasn't interested in nit-picking details. There was only one message he wanted to hear. The monasteries weren't fit to keep their wealth. He'd be quite happy to take it off their hands.

As usual he dressed up his greed in fine words. . .

I will make such a reformation that in the end I shall be eternally remembered in all Christendom.

Henry was right. He was certainly remembered. But more as a hooligan than a reformer. In 1536 he put the boot into the monasteries. They were condemned for their 'manifest sin, vicious, carnal and abominable living' – which roughly translated meant they were a dirty bunch of crooks.

Of course if they coughed up a lot of money, Henry might let them off – for a while.

Over the next three years, hundreds of monasteries were closed down. The monks were turned out and pensioned off. They were the lucky ones, nuns didn't even get a penny. The monasteries' animals and tools were sold off. Silver, gold plate and treasures went straight into Henry's greedy hands. Some of the monasteries were given to Henry's pals as manor houses. Others didn't survive hooligan Henry's 'reformation'.

The Hooligan's Guide to Reforming a Monastery

1. Find beautiful ancient building in peaceful countryside.

2. Dig under foundations and put in wooden props.

3. Set fire to props and watch the walls collapse.

4. Strip the lead off the roof and melt it down.

5. Invite local hooligans to loot the doors, windows and candles.

6. Take home monks' books as souvenirs. You may not be able to read but the paper is handy for other things.

Revolting subjects

The people of England soon grew sick and tired of Henry. They loved him when he was young and handsome and married to Catherine of Aragon. But once he kicked her out and took up with common Anne Boleyn, Henry's popularity took a nosedive.

There were other reasons for rumblings of discontent in the country.

1 Many loyal Catholics wanted Henry to end the split with Rome and bring back the Pope.

2 Many people objected to Henry looting the monasteries.

3 Both the rich and poor were fed up with paying heavy taxes for Henry's wars. One of Henry's new taxes was called The Amicable Grant or Friendly Tax. There was nothing very chummy about it – the tax demanded one-sixth of people's income.

The Friendly Tax was so unfriendly people attacked Henry's collectors and he eventually had to abandon it. **4** Finally the peasants were hopping mad over a practice called 'enclosure'. Trade in wool had become big business during the Tudor age and everyone wanted a piece of the action. So they started putting up fences on common grazing land to keep in the sheep. The King did it, the gentry did it, and so did the monasteries (at least until Henry pinched their land). For the ordinary labourer, enclosure was a disaster. One minute they were grazing their sheep in a green meadow, the next minute the meadow belonged to the King and their sheep had nowhere to go.

By the mid-1530s rebellion was in the air. Henry had lit the blue touch-paper himself by flattening the monasteries. It was the last straw. For the first time in 27 years of ruling England Henry faced a widespread revolt. The most dangerous rebellion was in Yorkshire, led by a one-eyed lawyer called Robert Aske. This is how Aske might have described the events that followed.

> Diary of a Yorkshire rebel
> October 1536
> By 'eck! The monasteries are plundered, the church disgraced, and poor folks are starving! I may only have one eye but I can see when

the country's in a proper mess. It's high time for them that's honest folks to rise up. I'll lead a peaceful pilgrimage in God's name. The King will give us 'is ear or I'm not a Yorkshireman.

WHAT CAN I DO FOR YOU, ROBERT?

November 1536

The whole country flocks to us! We swept through the north like a knife through butter! Every day there's rumours of rebellion and panic among them London rich folks. They say a grand army left London to meet us but the clodpoles left their cannon behind and had to go back!

One of our leaders, Sir Francis Bigod (a right hothead), wants to march on London. 'Hold fire, lad,' I told him. 'Our noble king will send us word soon.'

December 1536

I was right, tha knows! The King sent no less than the Duke o' Norfolk himself to meet us. If we pack off home in peace, we're all to get a right royal pardon. Henry promises to set up a parliament in the north to deal with our grumbles. A king's word of honour – that'll do for me! I'm off home to the wife and glad on't.

(Bigod reckons it's a weasely trick. Says Henry's just playing for time while he raises a bigger army. Like as not, Bigod wouldn't trust his own grandma!)

WHAT'S SHE UP TO?

January 1537

A month passed and nowt of the parliament we were promised. Our hungry lads grow restless. I hear that knave Bigod has attacked Hull and Scarborough with his men. He reckons the King's left us in the ditch. I cannot, nay, will not, believe it.

February 1537

Foul treachery! Henry has forsworn his promise! The Duke of Norfolk was sent north to punish us Yorkshire 'rebels' — no matter we'd kept the peace. Our poor lads were strung up like crows from branches. The monks of Sawley are swinging from their own steeple. On my way to London I passed bodies hanging all along the roadside. As for me, under arrest tha' knows. What's 'noble' Henry got in mind for me?

28 June 1537

Back in me own dear Yorkshire. Right kind of Henry to send me home, eh? He said he wished me family and friends to see me one last time.

YOU'VE BEEN ASKE-ING FOR TROUBLE...

Poor Aske's only crime was that he was *too* honest. Having never met Henry, he took it for granted that all kings kept their word. But Henry only kept his promises when it suited him. He was just relieved to have come safely though the worst scare of his reign. And all it had cost him was a few broken promises.

Witches and soothsayers

Rebellion wasn't the only danger that Henry faced in his reign. Once Henry lost his popularity, curses and spells began to rain down on him like hailstones. You might think an intelligent king like Henry would have scoffed at spells. But Henry was a Tudor and most Tudors believed in charms, potions, curses, prophecies and reading their star signs. Even Henry's cautious dad, Henry VII, was buried with (supposedly) a piece of the holy cross and a leg bone of St George. His son was equally superstitious. He crossed himself when it thundered and got in a sweat over storms in summer. Bad weather out of season was always a bad sign.

There were said to be 500 conjurers in England during Henry's reign, who would make magic potions and spells. Many more made their living from telling fortunes. Every now and then a brave or barmy person would cause a stir by predicting doom for the King. One of the most notorious soothsayers was. . .

Name: Mabel Brigge
Nickname: Fast Mabel
Speciality: St Trinian's Fast—
a murderous three days of
going without food which
leaves the faster's enemies
dead as a doorpost.
Criminal activities: Mabel tried her fasting trick
on one of her neighbours. Before the three days
were up she broke her neck.
Charge: The loathsome witch recently boasted
she is going to starve herself again. This time it
will be the king and the Duke of Norfolk
who get it in the neck.
Sentence: Execution. (Who's got it in the
neck now, Mabel?)

Noble magic

Of course, magic was important at Henry's court too. It was thought that anyone who rose to a high position must have used sorcery to get there. If Henry had started a Magic Circle, his entire court would have been in it.

Wizard Wolsey

Many stories were told about Cardinal Wolsey. As you may remember, Wolsey practically ruled England in his heyday. He was held in awe as the Mystic Meg of his day. Not only had he drawn up Henry's horoscope, it was said he'd used it to 'bewitch the king's mind and make the king dote upon him more than any lady or gentleman'.

Some believed that Wolsey had his own personal demon to do his wishes. Others reckoned it was a magic ring. A priest in Wolsey's service actually admitted having made a ring with a stone which could do marvellous things.

Vanishing Neville
William Neville was Wolsey's enemy and jealous of his magic ring. Crafty Neville paid a conjurer to make him a ring of the same kind. Not content with that he dreamt up a plan so brilliant it was stupid. Neville set to work to make himself a cloak that would make him invisible.

It's a pity we don't know what happened the first time Neville tried on his vanishing cloak. Maybe he thought he actually had become invisible. Given the magic recipe, his friends probably avoided him for weeks.

Mouldy Henry
Henry himself was the focus of one wild superstition. To simple country folk, the King was the terrible Mouldwarp, who the magician Merlin spoke of hundreds of years before.

The prophecy told of an evil king, who had a hairy coat, like a goat, and would. . .

. . .lead all his life in war and in trouble and in much strife.

According to the prophecy, the Mouldwarp ends up losing his kingdom in scenes of blood, gore and destruction. Castles crumble, rivers run red, the hills tremble and the Mouldwarp runs for his life like the hairy coward he is.

With Henry fighting rebels at home and enemies in Europe, many people were convinced the prophecy was coming true.

A tale of four Toms – Part 2
The last time we saw Thomas Cromwell he was knocking down monasteries. By 1540 it was his turn for the chop. Late in his reign, Henry saw enemies everywhere. He even suspected his friends of being his enemies. So it was no surprise when Taxing Tom fell out of favour. Someone had to take the blame for Henry marrying Anne of Cleves. Naturally it wasn't Henry's fault, so it had to be his chief minister's. There was one

small problem, though. Henry couldn't send Cromwell to the block just for suggesting an ugly bride. Even in Tudor times that wasn't treason. But that wouldn't stop Henry. He could always find reasons for another head to roll.

HENRY'S SECRET DIARY

10 JUNE 1540

By my oath! It's time to get rid of that rascally knave Cromwell. Funny how all my best advisors turn out to be traitors in the end. It turns out Cromwell holds dangerous protestant beliefs. By St George, I didn't know the fellow had any beliefs at all except making me money! But as a true Christian myself I can't have him spreading false teaching.

Yesterday I heard a story about Cromwell which made my blood run cold. It seems my chancellor once defended the teaching of Robert Barnes (a follower of that mad monk, Martin Luther). If anyone disagreed Cromwell said he 'would fight in his own person, with his sword in his hand against the king and all others.' To make his point he drew out his dagger and swore an oath.

The person who told me that story was the Duke of Norfolk. In truth Norfolk hates Cromwell like the devil himself and would gladly see him dead. But he wouldn't invent a story like that, would he? He kindly offered to go and arrest Cromwell himself right there and then.

12 JUNE 1540

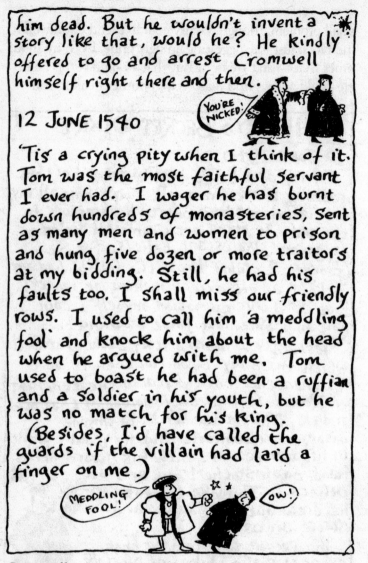

'Tis a crying pity when I think of it. Tom was the most faithful servant I ever had. I wager he has burnt down hundreds of monasteries, sent as many men and women to prison and hung five dozen or more traitors at my bidding. Still, he had his faults too. I shall miss our friendly rows. I used to call him 'a meddling fool' and knock him about the head when he argued with me. Tom used to boast he had been a ruffian and a soldier in his youth, but he was no match for his king. (Besides, I'd have called the guards if the villain had laid a finger on me.)

Cromwell was unprepared for his sudden change in fortune. He wrote to the King from his cell in the Tower. We can easily imagine what kind of letter it was.

FOR THE CHOP:

THOMAS CROMWELL

My lord the King,

There has been some grave mistake! Why do you keep me locked in the Tower? My only desire in life is to serve you faithfully. I would rather die than see any harm come to my king (though in truth I'd rather not die at all if it's all the same). My enemies accuse me falsely. (I bet it's that greasy villain Norfolk.) I beg you to consider how my words have been twisted.

Firstly, they say I spoke warmly of Robert Barnes' false teachings. True. But I spoke warmly against them. I warned my friends on no account to be taken in by such a lying serpent.

Second, I'm charged with vowing to fight against Your Highness himself, sword in hand. Not so! I vowed to fight sword in hand against anyone who threatened Your Highness. Surely you cannot doubt the great love I bear you. Remember how you used to clout me round the head and bellow playful oaths at me? How I long for those happy days again!

Lastly, I know you blame me for your unlucky marriage to Anne of Cleves. I admit I thought the match would be a useful one. Those German dukes have big ugly armies. How was I to know they have big ugly daughters as well!

There is an easy solution. Since it is Anne's head that offends you, why not cut it off instead of mine?

I beg for mercy on my bended knee.

Your humble, loving servant,

Thomas Cromwell.

PS Mercy, mercy!

PPS Mercy!

HENRY'S SECRET DIARY

25 JULY 1540

Fed up with Cromwell's letters from the Tower begging for 'mercy, mercy, mercy'. (Has the knave got three heads?) He used to send other men to the block without shedding a tear. Now he gets all weak at the knees when it's his turn! The traitor must die. He has committed foul treason against his king and master.

What was it Norfolk said he'd done again? I've got it written down somewhere...

Cromwell's pleas fell on deaf ears. The truth was Henry was in love again. This time it was plump little Catherine Howard whose uncle just happened to be . . . the Duke of Norfolk. This was good news for the ambitious duke but bad news for Cromwell.

Henry's new love didn't last long, however. Catherine was only 21 – but she already had dark secrets to hide. This was bad news for Uncle Norfolk and even worse news for Catherine. . .

The Tudor Tatler

13 February 1542

NO MERCY FOR KISS-ME-KATE!

It's too late for Kate

Young Catherine Howard knelt at the block today. Catherine, just 21 years old, had led a busy life. From the age of 15 she had flirted her way to the top. But in the end her kiss-and-tell boyfriends caught up with her.

Today *The Tatler* can reveal the shocking evidence of her scandalous life.

trusted her education to her step-gran, Agnes, Duchess of Norfolk. At the Duchess's house, the teenager was supposed to learn courtly manners. Instead she learned more about courting men!

Catherine attracted men like greenfly to a rose. Here is the list of the ex-queen's boyfriends:

Doting Duchess

Catherine's is a rags to riches story. Her penniless father

Henry Mannox

Manly Mannox was Catherine's music teacher at her step-gran's. He was employed to teach 15-year-old Kate the lute. He liked to liven up dull lessons by rewarding his pupil with kisses.

Mannox might have won Kate's heart if he hadn't been given the elbow by. . .

Francis Dereham

Flirty Francis was a gentlemen pensioner in the Duchess's household. That doesn't mean

he was past fancying young girls. Francis used to arrange secret midnight meetings with Catherine. They carried on their canoodling right under the Duchess's wrinkly nose. *The Tatler* has evidence that Francis and Catherine even went as far as getting secretly engaged. Their pet names for each other were 'husband' and 'wife'. (Hardly original but better than 'lovey-dove' and 'kissylips'.)

Thomas Culpepper

Hot Culpepper was a step up the social ladder for Catherine. He was not only a knight, but a member of the King's Privy

Chamber. Catherine's latest love introduced her to court circles. But Culpepper had to cool things off a while when Kate caught the eye of. . .

Henry VIII

Henry was still married to Anne of Cleves when he saw Catherine. He was desperate to ditch his ugly wife. Nineteen-year-old Catherine looked just right for his next port of call. She was young and lively, his *'thornless rose'*. Little did Henry know, he wasn't her first boyfriend and he wouldn't be her last.

Little and large

Henry fell head-over-heels in love with Catherine. It didn't matter that the 49-year-old king was old enough to be her dad. Not only that, he towered head and shoulders over his tiny bride.

Size doesn't matter

Catherine knew little about the ways of the world. Her family could have seen the danger in marrying the King. They might have mentioned the small matter of her list of ex-boyfriends. But they were too busy dreaming of the big palaces they'd live in. Somehow it must have slipped their minds.

Three weeks after his divorce, Henry married his young bride. For a short while they were happy. Henry showered his bride with emeralds, gold, clocks and crosses. Catherine had many of the gifts carved with her new motto:

'No other wish but his.'

(She didn't say which 'his' she meant.) Henry loved his dainty Kate. But he wouldn't have been so happy if he'd known what was going on behind his back.

Old flames

One of Kate's first acts as queen was to choose a secretary. Who could she have? Francis Dereham of course! Just the man, with his past experience of arranging meetings and writing notes. Kate herself was no scholar. Nevertheless she managed to write one letter in 1541. It was to another of her old sweethearts, this time –

154

Thomas Culpepper. *The Tudor Tatler* has obtained a copy:

> My dearest Tom
> I heard that you were sick and never longed so much for anything as to see you.
> It makes my heart die to think I cannot always be in your company
> Yours as long as life endures.
> Catherine XXXX

Haunting

Even as queen, Kate couldn't see why she shouldn't keep a few old flames burning. She was too young and headstrong to realize the danger of deceiving the King. Someone was bound to talk sooner or later. In the end it was a chamber maid at old Duchess Agnes's house. The rumours reached Archbishop Cranmer and turned his hair white. Cranmer passed the King a note at mass the next day. Imagine Henry's reaction!

Henry was out of his mind with rage and self-pity. 'We feared the King had gone mad,' said one courtier. 'First he called for a sword to slay her *"that he loved so much"*. Then he fell to weeping for himself. I believe he thought the whole court was laughing at him. Which was true of course – but only behind his back.'

The Tower

Catherine did her share of weeping too. '*It would have pitied any man's heart to have looked upon her,*' claimed Cranmer. But it was too late to

155

save her. One by one her old boyfriends were arrested. Francis Dereham was dragged to the Tower and tortured. Culpepper followed soon after. Both of them told tales on Catherine while on the rack. It didn't save their skins. Soon the Tower of London was so crammed with the Queen's 'friends', the royal apartments had to be used as cells.

Kate herself was terrified of getting the chop. She was so afraid of disgracing herself that she rehearsed her own execution! She had the chopping block brought to her cell so that she could practise placing her neck on it.

When the time came she was so weak she could hardly talk. Trembling, Kate confessed she deserved a thousand deaths for offending the King. Then she knelt at the block. Six years before, her cousin Anne Boleyn had knelt in the same place. Maybe in heaven the two of them can swap horror stories about marriage to Henry.

Scaredy Kate

THE TATLER COMMENT

So farewell Kiss-me-Kate. It was a short life but you made the most of it. Maybe someone should have warned you cheating on a king like Henry isn't a clever move.

We think you were hard done by. After all, you only had four boyfriends. Henry has had five wives and beheaded two of them, yet no one puts him in the Tower. We say 'Equal rights for queens!'

HAS-BEEN HENRY

Pills, wills and funeral bills

By the 1540s Great Harry had become Old Harry. Henry was in his fifties. Ask your grandad and he may say that 50 isn't old, but in Tudor terms Henry was a wrinkly. Henry hadn't looked after himself. He was certainly no muesli-munching health freak. Too much wine and red meat had taken their toll. What's more his body was paying the price of his early life. Regular jousting had left Henry with bumps and bruises all over. (He hung up his lance in 1536.) To put it mildly, Henry had gone to pot. Once it might have been whispered:

PSSST! THE KING IS FAT!

Now it was sniggered:

THE KING IS MASSIVE! A WALKING BLUBBER MOUNTAIN!

Henry's losing battle with the bulge was recorded by his court armourers over the years. In 1536 Henry was 45 years old. His chest was 114 cm and his waist a middling 94 cm. He was only a little larger than he was at the age of 23. Five years later just look at what had happened...

Even this wasn't Henry at his biggest. After his fifth failed marriage to Catherine Howard, the King went back to his old love – food. He ate until he could hardly stagger from the table. Soon even staggering posed a major problem for Henry. One courtier said he had 'the worst legs in the world'.

When he married for a sixth time in 1543, Henry chose Catherine Parr. Catherine was kind and sensible, not a flirty teenager like the last Cathy. She was 31 and no great beauty, but by this stage Henry was more in need of a nurse than someone to set his pulse racing.

In his last years Henry became a cruel, bad-tempered invalid. He mainly kept to the lower floor of his palace. If he did go upstairs he had to be hauled up in a hoist like a bag of cement! When his legs were bad he was carried from room to room in a specially made chair. Of course it was no ordinary chair. Besides being enormous, it was finished in gold velvet and silk. It also came complete with an embroidered footstool so Henry could rest his lumpy legs.

BURP

Tudor treatments

Stuck indoors, Henry's constant companions were his doctors and apothecaries (who supplied his drugs and medicines).

Having met Tudor doctors, you'd think Henry would have avoided them. Sixteenth-century doctors could be bad for your health. One of their favourite treatments was 'fustigation'. This meant the doctor took off his coat and gave the patient a jolly good beating.

Of course, Henry could afford the best doctors in the land. Court doctors were easy to spot by their long-sleeved fur gowns and black velvet caps: they looked a bit like hanging judges. They always carried bladder-shaped flasks at the ready and when the King went to the toilet everyone crowded around to inspect the results. Tudor doctors knew all about the royal wee. They liked to examine Henry's royal poos too!

Henry kept his doctors busy. In the past he used to complain of imaginary illnesses. Now he was *really* ill, he was a doctor's dream. His list of complaints was endless. . .

Plus his legs were swollen with ulcers, which later turned to gangrene so that the whiff of rotting flesh went with Henry everywhere.

To us today Tudor remedies sound crazy. They ate lettuce leaves for fever and swallowed lice for a bad liver, and Henry was willing to try anything. He even invented new drugs and medicines himself. One of his treatments was a plaster for legs swollen with ugly ulcers. By a lucky coincidence, it was just what Henry needed himself.

The King's Majesties Own Plaster.

1. Mix together marshmallows, linseed, oxide of lead, silver and red coral.

2. Add dragon's blood mixed in oil of roses, rose water and white wine.

3. Boil in a large pan.

4. Take it off the heat and let it cool.

5. Make into rolls wrapped in parchment.

6. Wrap the rolls around the swollen parts of the leg and wait for the ulcers to disappear!

Dead scared

Throughout his life Henry was terrified of dying. But in his last years his fears for his own safety drove him potty. Henry didn't trust anyone to lock the door behind him. He carried his own personal lock wherever he went. When he went to sleep at night it was fixed to his bedroom door. Once, at Allington Castle, he went even further. Henry got it into his head that assassins were out to get him. So he came up with a cunning plan to foil them . . . by sending for a bricklayer!

Every night he had his door bricked up so that no one could get at him. In the morning the wall had to be knocked down to let him out. Henry obviously didn't consider that they might decide to leave him inside!

UNBRICK ME AGAIN... I FORGOT TO CLEAN MY TEETH.

If murder didn't get him there was always disease. Henry was scared of all illness but his worst dread was 'sweating sickness'. The sweat was a fever that struck without warning. It was known in Europe as 'The King of England's disease', since only Englishmen caught it. In one London epidemic forty thousand people were said to have the disease. At the first sign of the sweat Henry fled in terror to the country.

Here's how a page of his diary might have read:

HENRY'S SECRET DIARY

I have made my will and confessed to a priest. Who ~~know~~ knows if I'll be next?

They say the sweat comes without warning. A man can be merry at dinner and dead as a duck at supper. You can be sleeping like a babe, then it creeps up on you in the night. You begin to sweat like a horse. You're hot and dizzy, you are dying of thirst – but you can't drink because then death is certain. The panic grips you. (I'm trembling just thinking about it!) The doctors say the first 24 hours are the worst. If you survive a day and a night you may live.

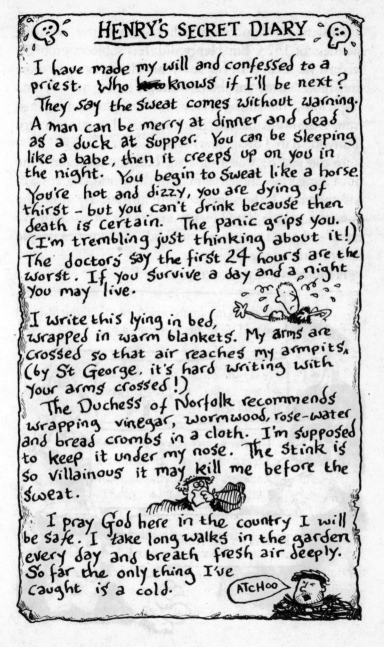

I write this lying in bed, wrapped in warm blankets. My arms are crossed so that air reaches my armpits. (by St George, it's hard writing with your arms crossed!)

The Duchess of Norfolk recommends wrapping vinegar, wormwood, rose-water and bread crumbs in a cloth. I'm supposed to keep it under my nose. The stink is so villainous it may kill me before the sweat.

I pray God here in the country I will be safe. I take long walks in the garden every day and breath fresh air deeply. So far the only thing I've caught is a cold. ATCHOO

Thousands of Londoners didn't survive the sweating sickness of 1528. But Henry did. His subjects probably wished he hadn't. In his last years Henry became more and more mean and bloodthirsty. He was moody and suspicious, imagining everyone was plotting against him. Often he sank into black moods, flying into a rage if anyone dared disagree with him.

In old age he was a bloated, bullying monster. 'The most dangerous and cruel man in the world,' said one of his subjects. Others went even further. By now the common people hated Henry and many of them didn't try to hide it. There were hundreds of reports of people bad-mouthing the King.

Here are a few that were recorded:

164

Henry's chopping list – the final years

In his last years, Henry's chopping block was kept busier than ever.

1 On London Bridge, heads and body bits are a common sight.

2 If the heads are taken down it's a bad sign.

3 Ordinary folk die every day for minor offences.

4 And abroad it's said...

In England death has snatched everyone of worth away or fear has shrank them up.

In all Henry had butchered two wives, a dozen or so of his own relatives and twice as many of his friends. That was just the rich and famous – hundreds of ordinary citizens were hanged or burnt just for stealing a loaf of bread or holding Protestant views.

Perhaps the nastiest of Henry's crimes was giving the Countess of Salisbury the chop. During her life Lady Salisbury had been like a mother to Henry. By 1541 she was a doddery old lady of almost 70. But that didn't stop Henry. He had her arrested and sentenced to death without a trial. Why? Just because her son had taken sides with the Pope against the King.

Will trouble

Soon it was Henry's turn to meet his maker. Before he died he made his will. It took care of his own burial and who should succeed him. Amazingly, though he married six wives, Henry left behind only three children. They were Edward, Elizabeth and Mary. Edward was only nine years old, Elizabeth was 14 and Mary a big girl of 31. Which of them would be chosen to rule the country?

Henry had no hesitation. It had to be little Edward. Nine may be young for a king but he was a boy. Like all Tudors, Henry reckoned girls weren't up to much. They certainly couldn't rule the country!

Henry's will said Edward would be helped to run the kingdom by 16 councillors while he was a boy. A brilliant plan? Put yourself in Edward's place. Would you have wanted 16 grown-ups telling you what to do?

What about the great hulk himself? Even to the end, people pretended the King would go on for ever. Henry spent his last months in a small room in his palace. Meanwhile his throne stood empty outside. But people were so scared of Henry they still behaved as if he was there. They bowed to the throne, removed their hats and even served meals to an empty table!

Finally, on 28 January 1547, Henry's great body drew its last breath.

The Tudor Tatler

Souvenir Issue 31 Jan 1547

KING'S DEATH KEPT A SECRET

Hang out the flags! Sound the trumpets! Dance in the streets! That monster monarch Henry VIII is dead at last. The King took his last breath in the early hours of Friday morning. But Parliament has been trying to keep it a secret for three days!

The King's close friend, Sir Anthony Denny, told our reporter, 'It's true. The King died days ago. We've been keeping his bloated body on his bed because we didn't know what to do.' The problem was the Duke of Norfolk. Henry had him locked up in the Tower waiting to be executed. He'd even signed the death warrant. But then the

King died first. 'That put the cat among the falcons, I can tell you!' said Denny. 'What were we supposed to do – obey a dead body or let Norfolk off? In the end we decided enough heads had rolled for Henry. Norfolk gets out today.'

in a tense finish

Bad fortune

Rumours that the 55-year-old king was dying have been the talk of the nation. But Henry, pig-headed to the end, refused to believe his time was up. Even the King's doctors could see he was on his way out (so it must have been obvious). But none of them had the nerve to say anything. The reason? Predicting the King's death is an act of treason. What if Henry revived and called for his chopping block?

In the end it was left to Henry's pal, Sir Anthony Denny to break the news. 'I told the King that "*in man's judgement*" he hadn't long to live,' daring Denny told us. 'Even then Henry didn't want to listen. He said he would have a sleep and think about it. When he woke up time was running out. We had to send urgently for Archbishop Cranmer.'

YOU'RE GOING TO POP YOUR CLOGS

Daring Denny breaks the bad news

Cranmer came hotfoot from Croydon. But he was too late to hear the King's confession (which should have gone on

169

for weeks!). For once Henry was lost for words. He hadn't the strength to speak, so he grabbed Cranmer's hand to show he trusted in God's mercy. A few hours later the King was dead.

Maud says 'Thank Gawd!'

THE TATLER COMMENT

Few of our readers will be sad to see Henry VIII go. Most Londoners were relieved when they heard the news today. 'Thank Gawd!' said streetseller, Maud Tyler. 'He was a foul tyrant and an evil husband to his poor six wives.'

'We are sick of seeing London Bridge used as Henry's head-stand,' said John Straw of Cheapside.

The Tatler agrees. Today we raise a mug of best ale to the end of cruel King Henry. May England never see as big a tyrant again.

Hero or monster?

Henry had started out full of promise. Where did he go wrong? Lots of theories have been put forward by clever clogs historians. Some say Henry was never the same after he fell off his horse in a joust. Others think he missed a mother's love when he was young. (Mum died when Henry was 11.) Most agree that the rot set in when he got rid of his first wife Catherine of Aragon.

But Henry wouldn't have seen the point in making excuses. In his mind he was always right. The treasures he left behind include a gold bracelet. On it is the motto 'To die rather than to change my mind.'

That sums up Henry in a few words. He had 100% faith in his own opinion. In an age when kings were like gods, Henry did whatever he wanted. He began at 17 by executing his dad's tax collectors and ended in his fifties by chopping off the head of his fifth wife.

By sixteenth-century standards, Henry wasn't unusually cruel. The reason we remember him is that he was always larger than life. Erasmus once called him 'the man most full of heart'. That was Henry, wholehearted whether he was hunting with his friends or hunting down his enemies.

Was he a bad king? Well it depends how you judge him.

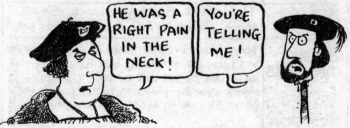

171

END OF TERM REPORT England 1509-1547 SUBJECT: Henry VIII CLASS: King	
RELIGION	Devious. Prepared to do anything to win an argument. Even start his own church.
BIOLOGY	Diabolical. Three children from six marriages is a poor effort.
ARCHITECTURE	Destructive. A sad waste of fine monasteries.
ECONOMICS.	Disastrous. If he'd paid as much attention to money as he did to fighting the country would be rich.
GEOGRAPHY	Deluded. Claimed to be king of France. Actually ruled a handful of French towns.
SPORT	Declined. A good sport until he let himself get out of shape.
ART	A dab hand. Thanks for the Holbeins!
LITERATURE	Dynamic. A king who wrote a book!
LANGUAGES	Deft. Being able to write Spanish, French and Latin came in handy for secret letters to Anne Boleyn.
MUSIC	Dedicated. Some good work. Shame about 'Greensleeves'. Such a lovely tune!
GENERAL COMMENTS	Henry has certainly made an impact during his term as monarch, but he wasn't the head boy he set out to be. Too often Henry thought pleasing himself was the same as looking after his kingdom.
TERM GRADE	5/10

Last laugh

It wasn't only Henry's kids who survived him. Two more of his relatives were there to see him buried.

Remember Anne of Cleves who Henry thought was ugly as a horse? She had the last laugh, by living on and on after her husband. At Mary's coronation she could be seen sharing a coach with Princess Elizabeth.

The other survivor was the last of Henry's wives – Catherine Parr. Although she'd been more a nursemaid than a wife. Nevertheless, she had to watch her tongue. Old Henry was still capable of one last trip round the chopping block.

In the end it was Henry who died. So the last word goes to Catherine.

Catherine Parr's Secret Diary

Goodbye sweet king! I can't say I'm too sorry you're gone. By the end you smelt as rotten as mouldy cheese. You can't complain, Henry, I did my best for you. I mopped your fevered brow and bore your evil temper.

'Saintly Catherine', 'Wise Catherine' they called me. But I was no saint, I was just fond of my own head. Especially as I was saving it for the man I loved.

Oh not you, my dearly departed. There was always someone else, right from the start. Did you not know!

In truth, being queen had it's good points. I found pretty clothes were much to my liking. The last queen (God rest her soul) had marvellous good taste. What luck her French gowns fitted me!

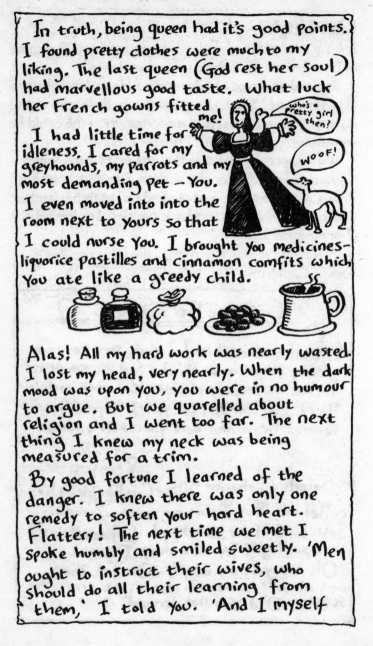

who's a pretty girl then?

WOOF!

I had little time for idleness. I cared for my greyhounds, my parrots and my most demanding pet – You. I even moved into into the room next to yours so that I could nurse you. I brought you medicines – liquorice pastilles and cinnamon comfits which you ate like a greedy child.

Alas! All my hard work was nearly wasted. I lost my head, very nearly. When the dark mood was upon you, you were in no humour to argue. But we quarelled about religion and I went too far. The next thing I knew my neck was being measured for a trim.

By good fortune I learned of the danger. I knew there was only one remedy to soften your hard heart. Flattery! The next time we met I spoke humbly and smiled sweetly. 'Men ought to instruct their wives, who should do all their learning from them,' I told you. 'And I myself have a special reason to wish to be taught by His Majesty, who is a prince of such **excellent** learning and wisdom.'

You still growled like thunder. 'Not so, by St Mary! You are become a doctor, Kate, able to instruct us and not be instructed by us.'

I thought quickly. 'Your majesty has much mistaken the freedom I took to argue with you,' I said. 'I did it to distract you from your pain, and of course to take the opportunity to learn from you myself.'

Your puffy old face broke into a smile and I knew that I was saved.

'And is it really so?' you said. 'Then, Kate, we are friends again.'

By heaven, I had passed close to death's door. The next day the Lord Chancellor entered with forty guards to arrest me! The knave had come on your orders, but he was much astonished by your greeting. 'Traitor! Fool! Vagabond!' you bellowed, as you drove him out of the room. It was all I could do not to burst out laughing.

And now it is quiet. Thou art gone, my

crusty old King. No more rages. No more threats of sending me to the Tower.

I can sit and write a letter now to my dearest love. 'Tis a funny thing, Henry, that you're his brother-in-law. His name is Thomas Seymour. That's right, you knew his sister, Jane. In truth, you were married to her.

Catherine Parr married Thomas Seymour in 1547, a few months after she buried Henry. Thomas was her fourth husband!